GAME OF
MY LIFE

INDIANAPOLIS

COLTS

MEMORABLE STORIES OF COLTS FOOTBALL

MIKE CHAPPELL

Foreword by Jim Irsay

SPORTS
PUBLISHING

Sports Publishing books may be purchased in bulk at special discounts for sales promotion, corporate gifts, fund-raising, or educational purposes. Special editions can also be created to specifications. For details, contact the Special Sales Department, Sports Publishing, 307 West 36th Street, 11th Floor, New York, NY 10018 or sportspubbooks@skyhorsepublishing.com.

Sports Publishing® is a registered trademark of Skyhorse Publishing, Inc.®, a Delaware corporation.

Visit our website at www.sportspubbooks.com.

10 9 8 7 6 5 4 3 2 1

Library of Congress Cataloging-in-Publication Data is available on file.

Cover design by Tom Lau
Cover photo: AP Images
All interior photos courtesy of the Indianapolis Colts

ISBN: 978-1-61321-908-9
Ebook ISBN: 978-1-61321-909-6

Printed in the United States of America

This book is dedicated to my No. 1 fan and the bravest, strongest person I've ever known, Angie. Hers is the brightest star in the night sky.

And to my wife, Cathy, who always has been supportive of me chasing my dream despite the late telephone calls from agents and interrupted dinners.

And to Matt, Becky, Ashley, and Johnny, and grandkids/future Colts fans Aaron, Levi, Luke, and Delaney.

And, finally, to my late parents, Dick and Evelyn.

CONTENTS

ACKNOWLEDGMENTS

I talked with Peyton Manning, Edgerrin James, Tony Dungy, Aaron Bailey, Marshall Faulk, Reggie Wayne, and all the others who had a "Game of My Life" to recount.

I helped them share their memories of a special time that is part of the very fabric of the Indianapolis Colts.

Shoot, I actually made deadline.

But I certainly didn't do it alone. Never have.

Anyone who has covered an NFL team for any length of time—I've written about the Colts since that inaugural 1984 season—owes so much to so many.

First, I must thank my wife, Cathy. She knows very little about the NFL but realizes my passion for it. She's tolerated the late phone calls and altered plans, the interrupted dinners, and my late nights in front of my laptop.

It's hard to put into words the influence my late parents, Dick and Evelyn, had on my career. They always thought what I did was special. I always thought I was just fortunate to have a job, one that I actually enjoyed.

And it's impossible to put into words the impact Angie had on my life and career. She took on leukemia for the better part of twenty-two months before finding peace December 14, 2007.

Finally, I want to thank the Indianapolis Colts in general and Matt Conti in particular for helping me bring everything together. The words of Manning, Edge, Wayne, and the rest are inspiring on their own. The photos provided by the Colts—I'm sure you remember time standing still when Aaron Bailey went up for Jim Harbaugh's Hail Mary—take them to another level.

Thanks to all.

FOREWORD

Through a half-century of life in the NFL, the game of football has left me with so many indelible moments. Football mirrors life. When we look back on our own lives, it's the unforgettable times that truly resonate with us.

The same can be said about my time with the Colts. Our history in Indianapolis began with a vision. Indianapolis and the state of Indiana have always done wondrous things. The Colts' beginnings in the Circle City started with building a stadium, the Hoosier Dome, when there wasn't even a team here. That was unprecedented and led us to moving here in 1984.

The inaugural season of 1984 included a miraculous home comeback victory over the Pittsburgh Steelers, one for the books. Three years later, we clinched our first division title with a memorable home victory over Tampa Bay; and nearly a decade later, the Colts and Steelers would once again meet in a nail-biting AFC Championship game that showed the rest of the league they would be dealing with the Horseshoe for a long, long time.

When January football rolled around for the next 20 years, the Colts set records for victories in a decade and consecutive seasons with 12-plus victories.

A new millennium saw the Colts embark on the winningest decade in the history of the NFL. The highlight came in the 2006 season. The New England Patriots were coming to town with a Super Bowl berth on the line. Down, 21–6, at halftime of the AFC Championship, there was no panic inside the home locker room. The greatest comeback in championship game history was capped two weeks later in the rain in Miami. Hoisting the Lombardi Trophy in the air was the ultimate dream come true. I was lifting it for the millions of Colts fans everywhere, signifying a team that had united a community over the years.

The memories haven't stopped there. Along the way, there was the thrilling one-point win over the reigning Super Bowl champion 49ers in 1995; and in 2003 in Tampa on national television, down, 35–14, with FOUR MINUTES REMAINING in regulation, Peyton Manning directed a comeback for the ages. Remember "4th-and-2" against New England in 2009? How about the historic playoff comeback victory over the Chiefs?

There are too many memorable games to recount in this Foreword, but there is one in particular I want to mention.

Indianapolis played host to perhaps the greatest Super Bowl week ever in 2012. After years of successfully hosting the NFL Scouting Combine and other major events, Indianapolis took the world's stage like never before for Super Bowl XLVI. The level of support that we have in our town is unparalleled. That's how we do it in Indiana. We take immense pride in our community, and there are so many people who have come before us who worked hard to make this city and this state very special.

The 2012 Super Bowl was something that is a tribute to all the people who have passed the torch in Indianapolis to make it such a great place to live and raise our families.

I am blessed to live and work in a very special community, and the memories are endless. And there are many more to be made!

Jim Irsay

He oversees one of thirty-two franchises in the country's most popular and lucrative professional sport, the NFL's Indianapolis Colts. When the team arrived in Indianapolis in 1984, Jim Irsay was twenty-four and the league's youngest-ever general manager.

Yet there were humble beginnings and lessons to be learned.

Flashback to 1972, when the Colts called Baltimore home and spent one summer in Golden, Colorado, for training camp. One afternoon, Irsay, thirteen at the time and the team's newest ballboy/gofer/grunt, ventured into the players' dining area. The crowd included so many franchise luminaries: Bubba Smith, Tom Matte, Mike Curtis, Jerry Logan, and others.

"I remember getting my food tray and sitting down and being nervous as hell with all those big guys—these heroes—standing around," Irsay said. *"And I remember getting a tap on the shoulder and someone said, 'Hello, son, my name's Johnny Unitas. Move your ass.'"*

Young Jim Irsay followed orders.

Now, more than four decades later, he's giving them.

Irsay assumed ownership in 1997, when his father, Robert, passed away. At thirty-seven, he became the NFL's youngest owner. Currently, his is a shared venture: daughters Carlie, Casey, and Kalen hold the title of vice chair/owner.

INTRODUCTION

The Colts have forged distinct histories in two cities, one of which wants nothing to do with the other. Understandable, considering Baltimore hasn't forgiven the late Bob Irsay—never will, for that matter—for uprooting its beloved Colts in March 1984 and trucking them to that basketball hotbed of Indianapolis.

We're not here to criticize Irsay. Nor are we here to applaud Indianapolis's movers and shakers for capitalizing on the disintegrating relationship between Irsay and Baltimore city officials to give the Colts a new home, the spiffy 60,000-seat Hoosier Dome.

We're here to chronicle the second chapter of the Colts' NFL life.

It's one that began with a geeked fan base that quickly was introduced to the realities of the NFL: a 23–14 loss to the New York Jets on September 2, 1984. Those of us on hand for that first step into professional football remember the epic quarterback duel. It was Mike Pagel versus Pat Ryan.

It intermixed occasional flashes—Eric Dickerson trampling the Broncos in 1988 on Monday Night Football, beating the defending Super Bowl champions in three consecutive seasons, the magical 1995 playoff run that ended with the oh-so-close Hail Mary in Pittsburgh that trickled off Aaron Bailey's belly—with too many losing seasons.

Then came 1998 and the arrival of Peyton Manning. Then, after that 3–13 start during Manning's rookie season, sustained excellence.

Yes, frustration continued to lurk, ready to keep Colts fans in line. They learned to despise Tom Brady, Bill Belichick, and the New England Patriots because they too often stamped out their playoff aspirations. Until January 21, 2007. Redemption was incredibly sweet and wrapped in a 38–34 victory over the Brady-led Patriots in an exorcising AFC Championship.

Throughout the years, the stars came out to play. Peyton Manning. Andrew Luck. Marvin Harrison. Edgerrin James. Dwight Freeney.

Robert Mathis. Reggie Wayne. Dallas Clark. Adam Vinatieri. Jeff Saturday. Tarik Glenn. And so many others.

Throughout the years, that collection lifted the Colts from just another NFL team to one of the NFL's flagship franchises. During one stretch, they reached the postseason in 11 of 12 seasons, including nine straight. They won at least 12 games in seven consecutive seasons, most in league history.

The overall picture is a montage of moments.

Finally clearing the Patriots' hurdle in the 2006 playoffs and using that historic comeback in the AFC Championship game as a stepping-stone to Super Bowl XLI and the franchise's first world title in more than three decades.

The utterly impossible comeback at Tampa Bay in 2003 that undoubtedly was among the most prized presents on Tony Dungy's forty-eighth birthday.

A meeting with the Patriots during the '09 season. Fourth-and-2. Enough said.

Manning's successor, Andrew Luck, pulling off an absurd Houdini act against the Chiefs in the '13 postseason.

Reggie Wayne willing the Colts to an emotional comeback win against the Packers in 2012 with his close friend/coach Chuck Pagano battling leukemia in a nearby hospital, stretching for the goal line with the game-winning touchdown.

So many personalities. So many moments.

We were fortunate to be on hand for each and eager to help refresh everyone's memory on what has made the second phase of the Colts' franchise so special.

As I rehashed those moments with those personalities, everything came flooding back.

I hope you enjoy the stroll through the past three decades.

I certainly did.

Mike Chappell
March 2016

CHAPTER 1

ANDREW LUCK

Quarterback 2012–present
January 4, 2014, vs. Kansas City Chiefs at Lucas Oil Stadium
2013 AFC Wild Card Playoffs
INDIANAPOLIS COLTS 45, KANSAS CITY CHIEFS 44

There was no avoiding the hype, or the comparison.

Andrew Luck wasn't replacing just any quarterback. He was replacing *the* quarterback—Peyton Manning, the face of the Indianapolis Colts since 1998.

Listen to Indianapolis Colts owner Jim Irsay after the team used the No. 1 overall pick in the 2012 draft to select Luck, the can't-miss All-America quarterback out of Stanford.

"All of the things that Andrew brings to Indianapolis and to the Colts are really special," he said.

Irsay had done his due diligence as the 2012 NFL draft neared. He quizzed league general managers and personnel experts regarding the worthiness and readiness of Luck to make the transition from collegiate star to franchise cornerstone.

"The comment you always got from them was, 'He is the best player I've scouted in twenty-five years. He is the top prospect I've graded for twenty years,'" Irsay said. "That sort of reputation of greatness has followed Andrew around, and he's handled it with so much humility.

"He probably doesn't even like me saying that, but it is true."

Notes on Andrew Luck

Joined Colts:	No. 1 overall pick in 2012 draft.
Jersey No.:	12
Birthdate:	September 12, 1989
Height:	6-4
Weight:	240
Games/starts with Colts:	55/55
Highlights:	Posted a 35–20 record in his first four seasons. Selected to three Pro Bowls and directed the Colts to the playoffs in each of first three seasons with 11–5 records. Led team to AFC Championship game after 2014 season. His 12,957 passing yards were the most by a quarterback in his first three seasons, while his 86 touchdowns were second to Dan Marino. Set club single-season record with 4,761 passing yards in 2014 and led NFL with 40 touchdowns. Established club records with eight consecutive 300-yard passing games in 2014, including 10 overall. Two-time Heisman Trophy finalist in 2010 and 2011 at Stanford. Started all 38 games and passed for 9,430 yards. Set school records with 82 touchdowns and 67 percent completion percentage.

Circumstances convinced the Colts to move on from the Manning era in March 2012. The team faced serious salary-cap issues with an aging roster, Manning was due a $28 million option bonus, and his future was very much in doubt. Four neck procedures forced him to miss the 2011 season, and Manning still was in the early stages of his rehabilitation.

Thanks for everything, Peyton.

Welcome to Indy, Andrew.

Luck did his best to keep things in perspective.

Was he concerned he had big shoes to fill?

"I think big shoes may be an understatement," Luck said. "What he did is, obviously, legendary for this city and for the state. I know that if I woke up every morning trying to compare myself to Peyton, I think I would go crazy. It's impossible.

"I realize that, so I am going to go out there and do the best I can. If one day I can be mentioned alongside Peyton in quarterback lore, it would be a football dream come true."

The early returns have been encouraging.

And most encouraging has been Luck's ability to replicate Manning's late-game heroics. He directed 14 comebacks in the fourth quarter or over-time during his first four seasons. Manning engineered a league-best 56 during his 18-year career, including 11 in his first four seasons.

Luck's greatest come-from-behind performance transpired in a 2013 wild-card playoff game against the Kansas City Chiefs. The Colts trailed, 31–10, at the half and 38–10 early in the third quarter before Luck led them to a 45–44 victory. It marked the second-biggest comeback in NFL postseason history. Luck passed for a career-high 443 yards and four touch-downs, and added a 5-yard touchdown when he picked up a Donald Brown fumble and stretched to the goal line.

The Game

By Andrew Luck

I remember that playoff game against the Chiefs. It was a late-afternoon game, a Saturday. There's always a good buzz. You can feel the energy. Great crowd. Raucous crowd.

We had a great first drive. We didn't score a lot of touchdowns on opening drives that year. There were constant questions from (the media) every week. "Slow starts. Slow starts. Slow starts."

On that opening drive, T.Y. (Hilton) caught a little inside post. Just a great route and we scored. It was great to start off like that. The Chiefs already had scored, so you're thinking, "OK, it's going to be a race track game."

Then, I wouldn't say it was a comedy of errors by the offense, but (the Chiefs) started rolling on offense and I started turning the ball over. It was interceptions. It was balls just a little behind guys, or trying to force a ball into a window.

We go in and we're down, 31–10, at the half. On our first drive (of the third quarter), Donald Brown had a free release, and I just threw it behind him (an interception by Chiefs safety Husain Abdullah). It was the worst possible way to start a second half when you're down like that. Just the worst, absolute worst, especially after all the adjustments at halftime and the time you put in to regroup.

Always the big points at halftime when you're down is number one, you can't do anything about what just happened. The score is the score. Number two, there is no 21-point touchdown. Just get positive plays and get back in a rhythm. I truly believe that. You have to as a player. And it's worked. We've come from behind a lot of times in the past. We did the year before.

Coach (Chuck) Pagano's mantra is play hard, don't look at the score-board whether you're up or down. I firmly believe that.

(Then he suffered an interception on the opening drive of the third quarter.)

It was like, "Great, here we go again." I don't want to say something clicked or there was an epiphany or something like that. There wasn't. But there wasn't much worse you could do as a quarterback.

After that (and trailing 38–10), we got into a real high-tempo, two-minute mode. We had two or three drives that were two and a half minutes. We had some big plays. Da'Rick Rogers went up and jumped for a post and caught it. Griff (Whalen) was making plays. T.Y. of course was catching everything. Donald Brown scored on a little trap.

A couple of (Kansas City's) guys got hurt, and offensively they slowed down a little. But our defense started creating stuff for us.

I remember Robert Mathis had that big strip sack. They were sort of in a four-minute mode, trying to run time off the clock. They had a play-action pass and it was vintage Robert Mathis, right? Off the edge, strip sack. That moment, to me, more than anything else was like (snapping fingers) "This is us. Rob's getting strip sacks." It just felt right.

(The Colts still trailed, 41–31, with 11 minutes to play when Luck picked up Brown's fumble near the goal line and stretched for a 5-yard touchdown.)

I remember it being a loaded box at the goal line. It's "OK, numbers-wise we really don't have enough players to block it." But sometimes you just let a Donald Brown make a play. We were going to stick our head in there and get the touchdown. Eric Berry made a great play. He just hit Donald perfectly, got his head right on the ball and it popped out. At that point, you just react. People made a big deal out of it, but I don't think it was a big deal. Anybody is going to pick up a ball that's on the ground and try to jump in. It worked out.

That's when you're thinking, "OK, maybe the ball is starting to bounce our way."

On the deep one to T.Y. (64-yard TD that gave the Colts a 45–44 lead), he ran a post and split the safeties. We were talking and both of us knew before the play we had a chance. He's the clear-out guy on that route. "Hey, clear it out and let's hit whoever is underneath." The other guy was primary underneath him. But the way the safeties had been playing, we left T.Y. at that place instead of moving him. We really thought there was a chance. He just ran, man. He did T.Y. stuff. He made a play.

We get ahead and then there's that fourth down that we stopped them. They threw a fade to Dwayne Bowe, and Josh Gordy made a great, great play. Perfect coverage. We were sitting on the bench and it was like, "Do I

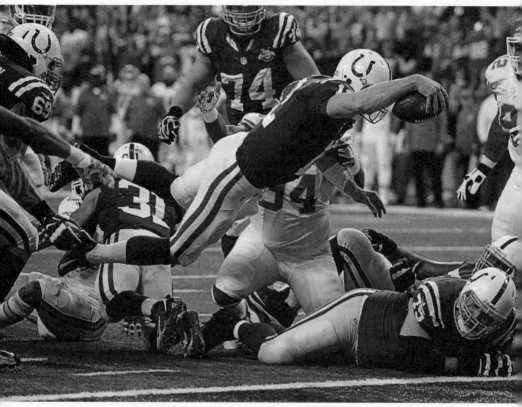

Quarterback Andrew Luck overcame a poor start, and the Colts chased down Kansas City, 45–44, in the 2013 postseason. Luck's 5-yard leap for a touchdown with a recovered fumble was a key play.

watch or don't I watch? Do I watch or don't I watch?" We watched. He made the play and we all were like, "Yes!"

People might find it hard to believe, but we never lost confidence in that game. I don't know if it was because what Coach Pagano went through (with leukemia) and the way he approached it. Maybe a little bit of that. But it also was the way he structures it, the environment he has created: just play hard and believe in the players. If there's time on the clock, you've always got a chance.

It's not like there were two minutes left and we were down, 38–10. We had time. We had possessions and we were a good football team.

There was belief.

The Aftermath

Exhaustion, relief, and a sense of accomplishment engulfed Luck and his teammates. They had achieved the nearly impossible by overcoming a 28-point third-quarter deficit.

"I don't think we thought of it as we just made the second-biggest comeback or climbing out of the biggest hole or anything like that," Luck said. "It was, 'Man, we won and we overcame a lot. That's great, and we're on to the next round.' That's what the playoffs are all about. It was time to move on.

"Looking back, a couple of years removed, you appreciate what we were able to accomplish. Right afterwards, you're relieved, ecstatic, all those things."

The euphoria didn't last. The following week, the Colts saw their play-off run end with a 43–22 loss at New England.

"Yeah, unfortunately we didn't keep it going that year," Luck said.

CHAPTER 2

PEYTON MANNING

Quarterback 1998–2011
January 21, 2007, vs. New England Patriots at RCA Dome
2006 AFC Championship Game
INDIANAPOLIS COLTS 38, NEW ENGLAND PATRIOTS 34

His was the fat résumé with the glaring void. He was the ultra-productive quarterback who saw an unflattering codicil attached to his recognizable name.

Peyton Manning was a two-time NFL Most Valuable Player and seven-time Pro Bowl selection. *Yeah, but...*

He opened his NFL career with nine consecutive seasons with at least 25 touchdown passes, a league record. He authored the finest season by a quarterback in league history in 2004, breaking Dan Marino's long-standing mark with 49 touchdown passes and eclipsing Steve Young's single-season standard with a 121.9 passer rating. *Yeah, but...*

Before Manning's arrival as the first overall pick in the 1998 draft, the Colts reached the playoffs three times in 19 years and never won more than nine games. In his first nine seasons, the franchise advanced to the postseason seven times and won at least 10 games seven times. *Yeah, but...*

Yeah, but Manning's Colts never seemed to have an answer in the playoffs. They were one-and-done four times, including in 2005 as the AFC's No. 1 seed, and never ever solved the New England Patriots.

Notes on Peyton Manning

Joined Colts: No. 1 overall pick in 1998 draft.
Jersey No.: 18
Birthdate: March 24, 1976
Height: 6-5
Weight: 230
Games/starts with
Colts: 208/208
Highlights: Announced retirement in March 2016 following decorated 18-year career. The NFL's only five-time Most Valuable Player, with the first four occurring with the Colts (2003, 2004, 2008, 2009). The only starting quarterback in NFL history to win a Super Bowl with two teams (Colts after the 2006 season, the Denver Broncos after the 2015 season). Named MVP of Super Bowl XLI, a 29–17 victory over the Chicago Bears. Posted a 141–67 regular-season record with the Colts and was 186–79 during 18 seasons. Including the postseason, his 200 overall wins are the most in league history. Holds Colts franchise records with 54,828 passing yards, 399 touchdown passes, 4,682 completions, and 7,210 attempts. Holds NFL all-time records with 71,940 passing yards and 539 touchdowns. Was named to 14 Pro Bowls, 11 with the Colts.

Manning's high-powered Colts reached the AFC title game after the '03 season, only to be silenced on a chilly, snowy evening in Foxboro, Massachusetts, 24–14. There was a rematch the following season in the AFC divisional round, and the result was the same: Patriots 20, Colts 3.

As the '06 AFC title game neared, Manning's critics dusted off their biting material. Colts coach Tony Dungy sprang to his QB's defense.

"I don't think you judge him until his career is over," he said. "I remember walking through the stands in Green Bay when I was a defensive coordinator at Minnesota, and people complaining after the games, 'We'll never win with this guy. He's too spacey. We'll never win. We have to get rid of Brett (Favre).'

"I can remember people talking about John Elway for years and years about how he wasn't able to win the big one. And after they win one, at the end of their careers, we canonize them because we realize how good they were.

"You've got to wait until it's over."

The wait for Manning and the Colts ended on January 21, 2007. With a trip to Super Bowl XLI on the line, they finally solved the Patriots.

The Game

By Peyton Manning

Obviously, we had come off a big win over Baltimore the previous week. After we won the Baltimore game, being a three seed, we weren't expected to be playing a home game for the conference championship. (No. 3 Colts won at No. 2 Ravens, 15–6; No. 4 Pats won at No. 1 Chargers, 24–21). When we found that out, it was obviously exciting. We had played well at home all year. Any time you're playing the (conference) championship at home with the chance to go to the Super Bowl, we were excited about that.

The game certainly did not start out the way we wanted it to. I remember we took some shots early. The times we had beaten New England up there in '05 and '06, we had taken some shots early down the field, and that was sort of our plan. We had hit those shots, so we tried it again this game. New England made a couple of good plays. Their two corners—(Asante) Samuel and (Ellis) Hobbs—made a couple of good plays on a couple of post routes to both Marvin (Harrison) and Reggie (Wayne).

We didn't get a lot going in the first half. We got a field goal. Samuel jumped a hook route in front of Marvin and ran it back for a touchdown to make it 21–3. That was not good at all. It did not look good.

I've always said when you're off to a bad start, sometimes it's worse to get off to a bad start at home than it is on the road, because the fans are disappointed and the players are frustrated. It does not look good.

I will say the last drive before the first half (ended), we did drive down there and get a field goal. I can remember we threw a fade route to Reggie into the end zone right before the half and thought we had pass interference. We really wanted to get a touchdown to make it 21–10. Referee had a no-call on that. Said they got their feet tangled.

But we did get a field goal to make it 21–6. I can remember at halftime, Coach Dungy being calm, like he always was. All he kept saying is, "Hey, two-score game. Good job getting points there. It's a two-score game. It's a two-score game."

That was our focus at halftime. It wasn't a good start, but we had still gotten it to a two-score game. The second half was up to us to get back into the game.

We came out playing well. Obviously had the two random touchdowns there. We hit Dan Klecko on a goal-line touchdown pass. We had a good drive to get down there. I think we hit Reggie on at least one big third-down conversion to keep the drive going.

The first drive of the second half was key. You want to build off of the drive at the end of the first half and don't go three-and-out, three-and-out, and give them a chance to extend their lead.

It was important to get off to a good start in that second half. Hit Klecko on the goal-line pass. He made a nice catch and was excited about scoring against his old team. He was our fullback on goal-line.

Our touchdown in the fourth quarter was when we thought Dominic Rhodes was going to score and (center Jeff) Saturday recovered that fumble. We thought that was kind of the football gods making it a wash because they had a similar situation where they fumbled and one of their linemen covered it in the end zone.

It's one of those times when you say, "Wow, maybe it's not our day." Then, sure enough, we had one where Dominic fumbled and Jeff recovered. Those kind of washed out.

After Klecko's touchdown, I remember Dungy had zero hesitation to go for two. That's all you want. You want your play caller and coach having a decisive plan. Right away it was "Go for two." We ran a play trying to hit Marvin on an out route, and they covered it pretty well. I ended up lobbing it to the corner of the end zone, and Marvin made a great adjustment to make that play for the two-point conversion.

On the quarterback sneak, we had some goal-line situation problems down there in a couple of the previous games. We got stopped down there. We had a fumble down there. I remember Jeff Saturday and me talking about if we got down there again, we're just going to quarterback-sneak it.

Seems like I hit Reggie on a quick pass just before that, popped it out and threw it to him to get us down there.

The fourth quarter had a lot of fireworks and a lot of big plays. Of course they were hitting some plays on offense. They had that crazy play where no one was covering that receiver (Reche Caldwell, split out wide right). Seemed like they had a touchdown pass where we pushed the guy out of bounds and they called him inbounds.

Dallas (Clark) was huge in the fourth quarter. Hit him on a couple of key corner routes deep on the left sideline. Hit him on a seam route for a big play.

Then we get down there on the last couple of drives.

We had a series before that last drive where we had a chance to go and do something with it. We changed personnel. We went to three wide receivers. (Brandon) Stokley had gotten hurt, so it was Aaron Moorehead, Reggie, and Marvin, with Dallas at tight end and just had a bad series. Just didn't do much with it. That was disappointing.

Quarterback Peyton Manning rallied the Colts from a 21–3 deficit to a 38–34 win over the Patriots in the 2006 AFC Championship game.

On that one bad series, I did hit my hand on (tackle Tarik Glenn's) helmet. It's one of those injuries where it can be an irritant to throw. You can't throw it quite as effectively. I had to treat it all two weeks before the Super Bowl. I remember telling (backup quarterback Jim) Sorgi to get loose. I hadn't thrown a pass yet, and all of a sudden you do and the ball is going every direction. That's not good. But I was able to throw. I was going back in.

We had that great stop (by the defense). Bob Sanders, boy, almost had an interception that would have changed field position. But they forced the stop. I remember on the first play of their series at the end, they had twelve men in the huddle, which was very unlike them. That forced them into a 1st-and-15, and we stopped them.

We get the ball back, and we decide to go back to two tight ends and two receivers. It was Marvin and Reggie, and Dallas in the slot. Dallas was doing a lot of his work in the slot. Then Bryan Fletcher at tight end.

You always want to get off to a good start on the drive. We hit Reggie on an out route and got a first down. They knew we were throwing it, and they were starting to bring the pass rush. We knew we had to throw on time.

This is when Bryan Fletcher was the one who said, "I think I can beat the linebacker on an out-and-up down the middle of the field." We tried that and they covered it. Incomplete pass. Then Fletcher, to his credit, was saying, "I think I can get open on a corner route." Interestingly enough, the coverage when they intercepted against Marvin on that hook route, they were kind of rolling their coverage to Marvin's side. Samuel had safety help on that play. That's why he jumped that hook route. By rolling coverage to that side, the safeties were away (from Fletcher's side), he had one-on-one coverage with no safety help.

Bryan Fletcher was right. A corner route was going to be able to take advantage of him with a linebacker with absolutely no safety help. We called the play to take advantage of that and hit Bryan Fletcher down the left sideline for a big play.

Then we hit Reggie on that play we always run, a little 5-yard under route. As he did so many times, he broke tackles and turned it into a big play. I got hit. We had the personal foul, so I knew we had a big play. That's when the ball got away from Reggie. The ball popped up. You talk about time standing still . . . the ball's popping up and Reggie's reaching for it and there's (Tedy) Bruschi and Samuel and it seemed like two or three others just around Reggie. They had their hands on him, and somehow he reaches up and gets it. Literally I can see the whole thing. I had kind of drifted that way. It was just frozen in time. How can this end this way? Reggie goes up and gets it back.

He gets that and we get a huge gain with the personal foul.

We got down there and we wanted to run some clock. (The Colts trailed, 34–31, with 1:53 to play.) We didn't want to score right away. We wanted to run the ball first, and we had a real positive run. We got about seven yards. That kind of changes your thinking. If you get three yards, you're probably going to throw.

At this point, we were just trying to get a little closer. We get to a 3rd-and-2 situation where we could run or pass. We ran that same running play again and Saturday had that nice block; everybody had great push. Because of the positive run on first down, we ran some clock and gave us some good options on second and third down.

Then Marlin Jackson had that great interception to end the game.

It was great team win. Any time you can come from behind at the end like that, against a good team and against a team that had knocked us out of the playoffs in two of the three previous seasons, that was special. Headed to the first Super Bowl, and to go on and beat Chicago was certainly a special time.

The Aftermath

Too many times, Manning had found himself facing his critics, explaining how another meeting with the Patriots in the postseason had gone so wrong. Not this time.

As confetti covered the floor of the RCA Dome, Manning hugged teammates and exchanged high fives. He savored a moment that too often had eluded him.

"It was a little nuts," he said of the postgame celebration. "It's not the normal routine after a game. You've got the on-field ceremony, then guys start getting back to the locker room at different times. Just an exciting time.

"I had friends and family up for the game. Eli was up at the game. It was one of the few times he was able to come to one of my games. I can remember driving out of the stadium, heading toward wherever I was going, and, boy, just the excitement of downtown. People were honking horns and celebrating. It truly was a celebration, not just inside the stadium, but throughout the city and I imagine throughout the state.

"It was fun to be a part of that. I know my dad still talks about the buzz downtown just driving wherever we were going. It was fun to be a part of it and fun to celebrate that night with family and friends and teammates."

CHAPTER 3

MARLIN JACKSON

Defensive back 2005–2009

January 21, 2007, vs. New England Patriots at RCA Dome

2006 AFC Championship Game

INDIANAPOLIS COLTS 38, NEW ENGLAND PATRIOTS 34

In arguably the most significant game in the Colts' Indianapolis era, Marlin Jackson delivered the defining play.

He picked off Tom Brady with everything on the line. His interception with 16 seconds remaining secured a 38–34 victory over New England in the 2006 AFC Championship game. Next stop: Super Bowl XLI and the franchise's first world championship in more than three decades.

No sooner had Jackson stepped in front of Patriots tight end Ben Watson than the RCA Dome was transformed into a confetti-filled snow globe. He immediately slid to the ground and was covered by teammate Robert Mathis.

Jackson had done his homework. Not only had film study prepared him for the greatest moment of his sporting life, it taught him how to handle it. Rather than look for a long return, he looked for the ground.

The previous week, the San Diego Chargers led New England, 21–13, with eight minutes to play in an AFC divisional game. The Patriots were driving, but Chargers safety Marlon McCree intercepted a Brady pass that

---

Notes on Marlin Jackson

Joined Colts:	First-round draft pick in 2005, 29th selection overall.
Jersey No.:	28
Birthdate:	June 30, 1983
Height:	6-0
Weight:	196
Games/starts with Colts:	56/32
Highlights:	Versatile defensive back during five-year career with the Colts. Registered 306 tackles, four interceptions, and 12 defended passes in 56 regular-season games. Produced arguably the signature play during the Colts' Indy era with an interception of a Tom Brady pass in the closing seconds that secured the 38–34 win over the New England Patriots in the 2006 AFC Championship Game. Colts went on to win Super Bowl XLI. Promising career shortened by three major injuries in 2008, '09, and '10.

---

could have essentially ended the game. But while trying to pick up extra yardage, McCree fumbled and the Patriots recovered. Given a reprieve, they drove for the tying touchdown with 4:41 to play, then won it on Stephen Gostkowski's 31-yard field goal with 1:10 remaining.

Jackson watched, learned.

"After I picked the ball off," he said, "I got down on the ground. That was from what I saw on tape from the previous week. The game was over, then

(McCree) intercepted the ball and fumbled. From seeing it over and over and storing it in your mental bank, you naturally do it when the time comes."

That time came, and Jackson seized the moment.

It presented itself with the Colts leading, 38–34, and 24 seconds remaining, and with the Brady-led Patriots facing 1st-and-10 at the Colts' 45-yard line. They needed a touchdown.

The Game

By Marlin Jackson

I remember them driving down the field. I remember the formation and my recognition and realizing what they usually run in that set. Then, just being able to diagnose that and getting myself in my normal alignment, maybe back up a little deeper so I don't have to drop and I can just read the quarterback and make a break with no wasted motion.

I already knew Brady liked to throw blindly. He would look one way, then throw blindly the opposite way. My pre-snap recognition within the play, I realized he's immediately looking the other way. I knew he was going to come back my way, so I had to be prepared, ready to break. I was able to make that play because of my pre-snap recognition and my film study and understanding my opponent.

Marlin Jackson (28) authored arguably the most significant play in Indianapolis Colts history when he sealed the 2006 AFC Championship game win with an interception of Patriots quarterback Tom Brady.

I was playing nickel corner and we were in cover-2. I was the seam defender. Usually the seam defender relates more to (the second receiver). They were in "trips" formation with two receivers to my side. It was Troy Brown in the slot and Ben Watson was the tight end. I knew they liked to hook him up around the hash marks or just inside of them trying to get a dink and dunk.

When (Brady) turned his head back the other way, I was like, "I was right." I immediately took off and made the play. I was talking to a DB the other day and told him about my anticipation, and when you see the quarterback's arm coming up and the ball's coming out, don't wait until the ball's gone to break on the football. If you see the highlight, you can see as soon as he turns his head back and cocks his arm back and his arm's coming forward, I'm going forward. That's what your anticipation from the film study allows you to do.

I backed myself up a little bit farther, looking like I'm out of the play and looking like I'm relating more to No. 2 (receiver), and the whole time I understood they were probably going to go to that player (Watson). I was able to back up and just sit there and read the quarterback and anticipate and go.

It was all film study and making a calculated, educated guess. After I picked the ball off, I got down on the ground. That was from what I saw on tape from the previous week when they were playing the San Diego Chargers.

That was the highlight of my career. How could it not be? That easily was the greatest sports accomplishment individually that I was able to make and have as part of my record.

I kept the football. It's in a closet, still wrapped up in plastic. Once I get my man cave together, I'll place it in there. I don't have that quite together yet. My son wants to play with it. He's asked to see it numerous times. I initially let him see it, but he wanted to throw it around. I told him, "Nah, that's not one you can play with like that." I'll take care of that one.

The Aftermath

No one should begrudge Jackson for occasionally wondering "What might have been?"

He was the Colts' 2005 first-round draft pick. He brought versatility to the secondary, dividing his 32 career starts among left cornerback, right cornerback, and safety. The interception that turned away the Patriots and Brady was supposed to be one of Jackson's many career highlights.

"I feel like I had the potential to create more of those moments," he said, "but obviously things didn't go that way.

"From time to time you think about (what might have been). It's just human nature, especially when I thought at that time I was really starting to establish myself. I was on the upswing of my career and on the path to reaching my potential."

Jackson started all 16 games in '07, but his '08 season ended after seven games when he tore the anterior cruciate ligament in his right knee. His '09 season ended after four games when he tore his left ACL. Each injury came during the relatively controlled atmosphere of practice, not amid the mayhem of game day.

Jackson signed with the Philadelphia Eagles during the 2010 offseason, but misfortune followed. He never played again after rupturing his right Achilles tendon in a June minicamp.

"You just have to take the lesson that nothing's guaranteed," Jackson said. "I realized I had other talents, as well, and I've been able to take that same drive, energy, and passion and put them into something else."

Jackson runs his non-profit Fight for Life Foundation and is active in Indianapolis, where he targets youth in the community. He's also working with collegiate athletes who are making the transition to the professional level.

CHAPTER 4

TONY DUNGY

Head coach 2002–2008

**February 4, 2007, vs. Chicago Bears at
Sun Life Stadium in Miami Gardens**

Super Bowl XLI

INDIANAPOLIS COLTS 29, CHICAGO BEARS 17

To truly appreciate reaching the mountaintop, often it's worth considering the start of the journey.

With that in mind, consider January 4, 2003.

The Indianapolis Colts had transitioned from Jim Mora to Tony Dungy after their 6–10 finish in 2001. They sought new leadership and were eager to put recent playoff failures behind..In postseason appearances after the '99 and 2000 seasons, the Colts had been one-and-done participants, albeit competitive ones. They lost at home to the Tennessee Titans, 19–16, in '99, then dropped a 23–17 overtime decision at Miami.

Owner Jim Irsay had seen enough. He firmly believed Dungy possessed the wherewithal to guide his franchise to a Super Bowl championship.

The first Dungy-directed postseason step came on January 4, 2003, in an AFC wild-card game against the New York Jets in East Rutherford, New Jersey.

It was exponentially worse than the two previous losses. In fact, it remains the most lopsided playoff loss in franchise history: Jets 41, Colts 0.

Notes on Tony Dungy

Joined Colts:	Named head coach on January 22, 2002
Birthdate:	October 6, 1955
Regular-season record with Colts:	85–27
Overall record with Colts:	92–33
Highlights:	Selected as a member of the Pro Football Hall of Fame's Class of 2016. Became first African-American head coach to win the Super Bowl with 29–17 victory over the Chicago Bears in Super Bowl XLI after the 2006 season. Only coach in NFL history to lead his team into the playoffs in 10 consecutive seasons (seven with Colts, three with Tampa Bay Buccaneers). Overall victories (148) in 13 seasons rank No. 22 in NFL history. Winningest coach in Colts history (92–33). Led Colts to five AFC South titles and seven playoff appearances during seven-year stint. Colts won at least 10 games in each season, including at least 12 in final six.

"That was one of the most disappointing games I've been involved with," Dungy said. "I told the team before the game—I'll never forget it—I said, 'I'm not a betting man, but I would bet my house on us because I believe we have a better team.'

"And we lost, 41-nothing. I just couldn't believe it. I was disappointed, but I wasn't deterred."

Colts fans undoubtedly were struck with a *here-we-go-again* migraine. Meanwhile, Dungy remained fixated on the long-term vision he shared with Irsay.

"I knew we had the right formula and the right thing going and that we'd only get better," he said. "I know a lot of people didn't see it that way, but I told the team afterwards, 'Just stay together. This is going to be a good football team.'

"It just wasn't our day for a lot of reasons. We had to overcome a lot of things just to get there, but it was a really good beginning for us. In some ways, it made some guys more determined. That got us off to a great start in '03."

Heeding Dungy's quiet but undeniable leadership, the Colts advanced to the playoffs the next three seasons only to fall short each time.

Then came February 4, 2007, and Super Bowl XLI.

The Game
By Tony Dungy

I had been there in 1978 (as a player), but obviously this was twenty-eight years later. I was surprised how much bigger the whole event was, all of the things that were going on, and how much coverage there was. We were trying to keep it as normal as we could. We went down there as late as possible. Of course, that was a big brouhaha with the media, why we came down so late.

We were coming off the big win over the Patriots, so it was good to have two weeks (before the game). I remember thinking it would have been tough for us to play again right away. But we got to relish that victory for the next couple of days. We tried to get going that next Wednesday after the game. We had Monday and Tuesday to enjoy it. But it was, "Hey, Wednesday let's get our focus back."

We were able to put (the Patriots game) behind us and think about Chicago. It was good in a lot of ways we were playing them, because their defense was so similar to ours. We could practice against ourselves. It was like our offense going against Chicago's defense. They were able to get a lot of good work in and really get started. That really helped our preparation.

One of the key moments for us is we had about four or five guys who had been to Super Bowls before. I had Anthony McFarland, Ricky Proehl, and Adam Vinatieri talk to the team about going and positives and negatives, the dos and don'ts. Ricky was just unbelievable because he was able to talk from both sides (winning and losing). He said you don't want to be the team that loses the game there, just how devastating that was. I think that really caught our guys' attention.

Our focus was pretty good all week. It was "Take advantage of this. Make sure we win the game, then we'll enjoy the aftermath."

As we prepared for the game, we talked about how we were going to handle Devin Hester. (Special teams coach) Russ Purnell had told us two weeks, "Hey, this guy is a threat, he's their biggest threat. Offensively they're going to have trouble scoring. We have to keep the ball out of his hands and make sure he doesn't do any damage, and we're going to be good." We practiced for ten to twelve days, angle kicking, squib kicking, all that. See how the wind is and if we thought we could kick a touchback, we'd do that. If not, we kick away from him.

Either the Friday or Saturday before the game, I started thinking about it. "We're at the Super Bowl. We can't play afraid. We've got to kick it down the middle and show them that we're here to win the Super Bowl." At the very last minute, I changed. I told the team, "I hope we lose the toss, because we want to kick off and pound their best weapon. It'll send a message."

I don't know why I came up with that decision, but I did. We lost the toss and we kicked off to him and he took it all the way in (92-yard touchdown). I remember thinking after he scored, "Well, that wasn't a very good decision."

But the college football championship game had started the same way. Ohio State was playing Florida and Ted Ginn took the opening kickoff back to the house for Ohio State, then Florida just dominated from there on out. I remember thinking, "Hopefully this game turns out the same way."

It was a rough, rough start. None of us felt very good about it. But we had been through so much that year, the ups and downs, the 44–17 (loss) at Jacksonville. Guys weren't going to get rattled by one play or one moment.

After the kickoff, I felt like we controlled the game. It was funny, because we were behind quite a bit. We were down, 14–9 (in the second quarter), but I just felt like we were winning the game. We were doing so much right. We were doing everything we needed to do, other than the opening kickoff and one long run.

We knew the game was going to be that way. I remember talking with Peyton in the weeks leading up to it. "They're going to play this (type of defense), they're going to give us six-man fronts and seven-man fronts. They're going to try to take away the wide receivers and challenge us to be patient and run the ball." I said, "I coached this defense." If people are patient, you can be methodical and that's what we'll have to do.

Joseph Addai and Dominic Rhodes were just outstanding. If I were voting, I probably would have split the (MVP) between those two backs. We knew we were going to have to be patient and run the ball, and they were such a big part of the game.

It was a game where we were going to have to do that. We were going to have to throw to the tight ends. They had one broken coverage where Reggie got the long touchdown, but the majority of the game was underneath throws, hitting the tight end, running the ball, hitting the backs out of the backfield, and taking advantage of how you have to play against that coverage and that mind-set.

Other than the fumbles we had, it was a pretty good game for us.

We were ahead, 22–17 (in the fourth quarter), and that was hard to believe. You're sitting there feeling like you've done everything you wanted to do, and if they hit one play, they're back ahead. And then Kelvin Hayden came up with the big play.

I was right in front of Kelvin, probably 10 yards away, when he caught the ball. They were coming at us. I was at the far end (of the bench), so I could watch. The ball came right to us and I saw him. I was sure it was a catch, and I was sure it was a catch inbounds. But I didn't know if he stepped out or not. At the Super Bowl, they had the alternate officials. One guy was right with us. He was on our sideline, and I said "I don't think he stepped out of bounds." He said, "No, I don't think he stepped out, either." So we're both just there waiting for the replay.

It was something we practice a lot. He went up the near sideline and we got all the blocks (on a 56-yard interception return for the clinching touchdown). It was just the way you practice it. To have Kelvin make that play just cemented our philosophy that everybody has to be ready to go. Nick Harper went as long as he could go and at halftime told us he didn't think he could be effective in the second half.

Kelvin stepped in and he was ready. That's what we preached all year. Be ready, and when your time comes, make a play. We had so many examples of that all season. That's what made the game and that season so special. Our 2006 team probably was not as physically talented as our '05 team, but it found so many ways to win games. Marlin (Jackson) making that big interception and Bryan Fletcher making that big catch on the game-winning drive (in the AFC title game versus New England). Kelvin Hayden in the Super Bowl. Dominic getting 100 yards in a backup role. Joseph had been the backup all year, and then we started him in the playoffs.

It was that type of team. Everybody made a contribution. It was special.

The Aftermath

The South Florida rain continued to fall, but no one seemed to notice. Dungy was given the obligatory Gatorade dousing, and he, Manning, owner Jim Irsay, and so many others pierced the night sky by hoisting the shiny Lombardi Trophy.

"It's pretty special," Dungy said. "For me, I just remember looking around at all of our people. By that time, the Chicago people start to file out of the stadium. The stadium's not full like it was after the AFC Championship Game (in Indianapolis), where everybody stayed.

"You look, and these are our guys. You see the families start to come on the field, and the players. You realize it was a team win, a win for the city, a win for all of our fans.

"It was really a satisfying moment to realize we had climbed the mountain and we made it."

Tony Dungy became the first African-American head coach to win a Super Bowl when the Colts defeated the Chicago Bears in Super Bowl XLI after the 2006 season.

At some point, the historical magnitude took hold. No other African-American head coach had found himself in this position.

"It was pretty neat, pretty special," Dungy said. "I watched all the Super Bowls and I remember thinking when the Redskins won with Doug Williams what a neat moment that was.

"I knew the significance. I thought back to so many of the coaches when I was young that I watched that could have done it if they had had the opportunity. To have the opportunity, to win it, to be there with Lovie (Smith, Bears coach) and know that I had hired him into the NFL, and there we were.

"It was a gratifying thing."

Dungy thought of his first conversation with Irsay after the 2001 season. He had been fired by the Tampa Bay Buccaneers and was considering his options, which expanded to the Colts when Irsay called.

What struck Dungy the most was Irsay's message.

"I had had a couple of people calling me about head coaching," he said. "But when he called me, he said, 'I want to build this the right way. We want to connect with our fans. We want to be the right people in the community. We want to win, but we want to do more than that.'

"I knew this was a guy who believed exactly what I believed and we're going to be in lockstep and it's going to be good."

It turned out to be Super.

CHAPTER 5

REGGIE WAYNE

Wide receiver 2001–2014

October 7, 2012, vs. Green Bay Packers at Lucas Oil Stadium

INDIANAPOLIS COLTS 30, GREEN BAY PACKERS 27

Theirs was a friendship born in Coral Gables (Florida), nurtured on the competitive practice fields at the University of Miami and deepened by a reunion and hardship in Indianapolis.

Reggie Wayne was a two-time all-state wide receiver from John Ehret High School in Marrero, Louisiana. In 1997, he was among the next wave of talent to boost the Hurricanes' roster. Chuck Pagano, whose roots reached back to Colorado and Wyoming, coached Miami's secondary and special teams.

"He didn't recruit me, but our relationship was super close because we had so many one-on-one battles, receivers versus DBs throughout the week," Wayne said.

Wayne's roommate was safety Ed Reed, an integral member of Pagano's secondary who eventually will have a bust in the Pro Football Hall of Fame. They would hang together off the field, push each other on it under Pagano's watchful, motivating direction.

"Chuck was also the special teams coach," Wayne said. "We all played special teams. We just got tight throughout the years and years and years.

"When he went to Baltimore (as a Ravens defensive assistant), we always would stay in contact. It's a 'U' thing. It's a Miami thing. That's what you do. We are family."

That family unit tightened in 2012. In January, Pagano was named the Indianapolis Colts head coach. One of his first phone calls was to Wayne, whose contract with the Colts was expiring, making him an unrestricted free agent.

"His exact words were 'I can't do this without you,'" Wayne said. "I was like, 'OK.' He had just got the job, and I called him to congratulate him because I was happy for him. I didn't call to talk about me or anything like that. I knew he was going to a great organization. I knew his wife. I knew his daughters. I knew they were going to love Indianapolis.

"He said, 'What are you up to?' I told him, 'I'm getting ready for this free agency thing.' He said, 'I just want you to know I'm excited to be here, to be head coach of this football team. I want you to know I can't do this without you.' I'm like, 'I'm not ready to start coaching just yet.' He kept saying, 'I need you on this team. I need you on this team.' That's all he had to say."

Then came the bombshell. Pagano revealed on September 26, 2012, that he had been diagnosed with acute promyelocytic leukemia (APML). He went on indefinite leave while undergoing treatment at the IU Health Simon Cancer Center. Bruce Arians, his close friend and offensive coordinator, served as interim coach.

"Crushed," Wayne said of his reaction, and that of his teammates.

But everyone moved forward. The first step on the football field came less than two weeks after the diagnosis against the Green Bay Packers at an emotional Lucas Oil Stadium.

"We went out and played for Chuck," said Wayne.

He wore orange gloves in recognition of Pagano's battle with leukemia. He finished with 13 receptions for a career-best 212 yards. His 4-yard touchdown with 35 seconds remaining was the difference in a 30–27 victory.

Notes on Reggie Wayne

Joined Colts:	First-round draft pick in 2001, 30th overall selection
Jersey No.:	87
Birthdate:	November 17, 1978
Height:	6-0
Weight:	203
Games/starts with Colts:	211/197
Highlights:	Ranks second in franchise history with 1,070 receptions, 14,345 yards, and 82 touchdowns. Receptions rank No. 7 in NFL history, while the yardage ranks No. 8. Set franchise records by appearing in 211 regular-season games and participating in 143 victories. Holds single-game record with 15 receptions against Jacksonville in 2010 and ranks No. 3 with 212 yards against Green Bay in 2012. Established franchise playoff records with 21 games, 93 receptions, 1,254 yards, and nine touchdowns. Receptions rank No. 2 in league history behind Jerry Rice (151), and yards rank No. 4 behind Rice (2,245), Michael Irvin (1,315), and Cliff Branch (1,289). Selected to six Pro Bowls and was first-team All-Pro in 2010. Led team in receiving in six straight seasons from 2007–12, tying Marvin Harrison's team record. Four-year starter at the University of Miami. Set school records with 173 receptions and had 20 touchdown catches, joining Lamar Thomas and Irvin as the only Hurricanes with at least 20 in a career.

The Game
By Reggie Wayne

Best game of my career. The best, and I played somewhat with a heavy heart. Just with my relationship with Chuck, I knew there was no way we could come out of this game with a loss. We were down pretty good early, 21–3 or something like that, but it was one of those games where you wanted to refuse to lose.

The majority of the game I was going up against Charles Woodson, who I played maybe three times in my career. Every time I left the game against him, I felt like he got the best of me. That was another challenge I had going into that game. You had the whole thing with Chuck, and it was Bruce Arians's first game as head coach. All the players had so much respect for Chuck.

It was one of those games where once you got the ball in your hands early, you got in a zone and just kept going. It felt like no matter where the quarterback threw the ball, you were going to catch it. You felt like if he could get it anywhere within a mile's radius . . . I was in such a zone I felt like I could catch a BB in the dark.

I wore the orange gloves in honor of Chuck and his battle with leukemia. It was playing with a heavy heart. We always say you never ask "Why?," but that was kind of a hard question to avoid when you have something like that and you're going through tough times like that. In my mind, I just wanted to go out there and do it for him.

We got behind (21–3 at the half), and I honestly believe everyone was still in shock from what was going on even though we had the whole week to get it going. I remember Bruce Arians was in the team meeting, and he put Green Bay's top five guys up on the board. There was Aaron Rodgers, Charles Woodson, other guys. He had Green Bay's top five guys up there. Then he had pictures of our top five guys. It was Andrew Luck, it was myself, it was Robert Mathis. He said the team that wins is going to be the team whose best five guys win. "We need our top five guys to beat their top five guys." So, that's another challenge I'm facing. I'm into the game and it's like, "Damn, you're putting me as one of the top five guys on the team and I'm going against Charles Woodson, who I've never had a good game against. And on top of that I've got one of my closest friends that I've known for sixteen years battling leukemia who ended up being the coach of the team I'm playing for."

At halftime, we knew we hadn't played our game. But we all challenged ourselves: "OK, we got that out of our system. These are the cards we've been dealt. You're either going to fold or you're going to play your hand." Everybody was finally able to relax a little bit and lock in and play ball.

Playing at home, we knew all 65,000 people knew what was going on with our head coach. It would have been easy for us to hang our heads, and everybody would have understood that the Indianapolis Colts were going through tough times right now with their coach down. That's the road we were taking in the first half. But as men, we didn't want to live with that excuse. We all challenged ourselves at halftime.

I don't know if it was the orange gloves or what, but it seemed like every time Andrew dropped back, he threw it to me. It was definitely a game where I gave it everything I had.

The play that turned the game around was Jerraud Powers's interception in the third quarter. We knew that Aaron Rodgers was the king of back-shoulder fades, and we worked on that. I remember me and Jerraud practicing that all week during our one-on-one sessions. He wanted to work against the back-shoulder fades so he could get the look. It's awesome when you see something you'd been working on and working on come to light. That play changed the whole structure of the game. I don't think we let go of the momentum the rest of the game.

(Packers still led, 27–22, with 4:30 remaining. On the ensuing game-winning drive, Wayne had five catches for 64 yards, including the 4-yard touchdown.)

A lot of people call that last drive the "Reggie Drive." I'll take that. I remember Donnie Avery coming up to me because it was a timeout. He said, "Hey, it's your time. We need to keep throwing you the ball. You do what you do." It was one of those things where you're locked in. It didn't matter. I couldn't have done it without my teammates, but man, it was something that had to happen. When it was all said and done, when it was all zeroes on that clock, I just wanted to make sure that everybody knew 87 left it all on the field for various reasons. And the biggest reason was Chuck.

Wide receiver Reggie Wayne capped an emotional come-from-behind victory over the Green Bay Packers with a stretching 4-yard touchdown pass with 35 seconds remaining in the Colts' 30–27 victory.

Everything fell into place. The O-line gave Andrew Luck time to throw, the defense stepped up when we really needed it to. We all did what we had to do. It was special.

I remember everything about the touchdown. It was a blitz-adjustment where they blitzed off the edge, and I was in a stacked position to the left. I actually hate that play. It's one of those things where you're reading "hot" (blitz) and you're adjusting to your hot read and Luck's going to get it to you right now. But when you catch the ball, you understand you're going to get whacked. You're in the middle of traffic.

They line up and they're showing blitz early. I'm thinking, "Please don't blitz. Please don't blitz." He blitzes off the edge, I adjust my route, Luck throws it to me, and Tramon Williams is standing right there. As soon as I catch it, he grabs me. He has me around my legs and my hip area. I'm a true believer that you mess up and fumble when you try to do too much. I can see the end zone, the goal line. I can see it. But I know people are coming. Something just said, "Just reach the ball out." And remember, everything's in slow motion.

I reach it out and I'm not sure if I make it or not. I gave it a quick reach. As I'm reaching, I can see two more defenders coming in. I honestly don't know if I got it in, but I'm lying on my back and I'm making sure I've still got the ball. I feel six arms grabbing me, trying to tackle me.

All of a sudden, the first guy I feel grab me is Andrew Luck. I'm on my back on the ground. If I'm a baby, I'd have had shaken baby syndrome. He shook me and kept shaking me. It was electric.

That probably was one of the only times I actually heard the crowd in the middle of a game. Normally, you're so locked in you don't hear anything. That right there, it was so electric.

It was a great game. Just the way we fought back.

It was for Chuck.

The Aftermath

There still was unfinished business.

Wayne had visited Pagano in the hospital on a few occasions prior to the game. Each was emotional. They paled in comparison to their meeting the day after the stirring victory over the Packers. Wayne presented his friend and coach with the orange gloves he wore during the game.

"I waited until Monday because he was in between treatments," he said. "He was like a little kid when I saw him. He enjoyed watching that game and he was so happy and appreciative of the way we played, that we never gave up.

"He didn't know I was going to wear the orange gloves. He understood the whole meaning of the orange gloves. It worked out perfect. He said, 'Every time I looked up, I just saw those orange gloves doing this, doing that.' He told me, 'You played great. You played phenomenal, man.'"

Wayne was gripping a bag that held the orange gloves.

"He didn't know I was giving them to him," he said. "I told him, 'You don't have to look at the screen to see those orange gloves because I'm hand-delivering them to you.' He probably won't enjoy me saying this, but the tears started coming out of his eyes. He started bawling and we hugged each other.

"It's family, man. It's family above all else. That's what the NFL is about. It's about the relationships you build. That lasts forever. It was a touching moment. We understand as players that we come and go, some sooner than others. But those relationships, that's almost like you won the Super Bowl. You can't take that away.

"That lasts forever. You take that to the grave."

CHAPTER 6

CHUCK PAGANO

Head coach 2012–present
December 30, 2012, vs. Houston Texans at Lucas Oil Stadium
INDIANAPOLIS COLTS 28, HOUSTON TEXANS 16

Everything changed September 26, 2012, for a family, an NFL franchise, and a community.

Chuck Pagano, the Indianapolis Colts' head coach for nine months, and wife Tina sat in an examining room at the IU Simon Cancer Center in Indianapolis and awaited a consultation with Dr. Larry Cripe. His message rocked the pair to the core: "You need to be in the hospital," Cripe informed Chuck. "You could die without effective treatment immediately."

Pagano had been diagnosed with acute promyelocytic leukemia.

"Such shock," Tina said.

Such perspective.

Three days earlier, Pagano stood on the sideline at Lucas Oil Stadium and thought it couldn't get any worse. His Colts took a 17–16 lead over the Jacksonville Jaguars with 56 seconds remaining when Adam Vinatieri knocked down a 37-yard field goal. On the first play of the ensuing Jaguars' possession, Blaine Gabbert hit Cecil Shorts III with an 80-yard touchdown that stunned the sellout crowd, the Colts, and their emotional coach.

"Obviously a devastating, devastating loss," Pagano said after the 22–17 shocker. "This one's going to sit in the pit of our stomachs for quite some time."

A professional setback quickly was replaced by a personal trial.

Pagano had been experiencing unusual fatigue and bruising for nearly two months but basically had brushed aside the warning signs as he directed his first NFL team through training camp and the first three weeks of the regular season.

Notes on Chuck Pagano

Joined Colts: Named head coach on January 25, 2012
Birthdate: October 2, 1960
Highlights: Succeeded Jim Caldwell as head coach in 2012. Joined Jim Harbaugh as the only coaches in NFL history to lead their team to at least 11 wins in each of their first three seasons. Colts were 33–15 in Pagano's first three seasons and are 41–23 in four seasons. His .641 winning percentage ranks fourth among active head coaches. Joined Ted Marchibroda (1975–77) and Tony Dungy (2002–04) as the only coaches in Colts history to take the team to the playoffs in each of his first three seasons. Colts set NFL record by winning 16 straight division games from 2012–15. Signed four-year extension in January 2016. Was Baltimore Ravens' defensive coordinator in 2011 and the team's secondary coach from 2008–2010. Other NFL positions included secondary coach with Cleveland Browns (2001–04) and defensive backs with Oakland Raiders (2005–06).

Fortunately, the bye week followed the loss to Jacksonville. Pagano put the team through early-week practices, and there was the annual team picture session before players scattered for a four-day weekend. He and Tina then met with Dr. Cripe on a Wednesday.

"I went down to the Simon Cancer Center, and when doc told me what I had, all I could think about—and I had about two seconds to digest it—was what Robert (Mathis) told the team in the locker room after the Jacksonville loss," Pagano said.

Mathis's message: There are no pity parties in the NFL. Everybody man up. Deal with it.

"So I'm sitting there thinking, 'There's no pity parties in life, either,'" Pagano said. "I've got my wife and three daughters and granddaughters. They're all counting on me.

"I told Doc, 'OK, give me the game plan. Tell me what I need to do to beat this thing.'"

Pagano went on indefinite leave—longtime friend and offensive coordinator Bruce Arians was named interim coach—and entered the hospital to fight for his life. He spent twenty-five days in the hospital and completed the remainder of his three-month treatment at home. Three rounds of chemotherapy drained his energy and took his hair. On the more difficult days, he'd sleep twenty hours.

"When they start putting that chemo in you," Pagano said, "they've got to kill everything. To get the bad (blood cells), you've got to kill the good ones."

Pagano kept in contact with Arians, his coaching staff, and his players through texts, emails, and phone calls. His goal was to return to the team before the end of the season. Arians made certain the light remained on in Pagano's office 24/7, until Pagano was able to flip the switch.

"All that time, Bruce kept talking about extending the season," said Pagano, who was released from the hospital on October 21.

Eight days after being discharged, he visited the Colts' headquarters and sat in as Arians discussed the upcoming game against Miami with his staff. He attended the Dolphins game, his first since being diagnosed, and addressed the players before and after the 23–20 victory. He subsequently attended home games against Buffalo and Tennessee.

Pagano watched the Bills game from a suite at Lucas Oil Stadium and drew a loud ovation when he was shown on the Jumbotron. He tapped his chest several times and mouthed the words "Thank you. Thank you."

Cripe announced Pagano was in remission on November 5 and cleared him to return to his coaching duties on December 24.

"You're away, you're away, you're away," Pagano said of his three-month hiatus. "You're watching and you're communicating, but you're not with them. You're not on the grass. You're not on the field. You're not in the meeting rooms. You're not in that stadium.

"But you know you're getting closer every single day to that day they actually tell you, 'OK, you're good to go.' Then you go back to work."

The Houston Texans were in town for the regular-season finale.

Chuck Pagano was back.

The Game
By Chuck Pagano

Christmas Eve was the day I came back to work. They had just beaten Kansas City on the road and clinched a playoff berth.

I can just remember walking into that team meeting and being back in the building and we had a presser right after. It was surreal. I remember talking with the team, and it was pretty emotional as you can imagine. I don't know how to describe it. Going through what we all went through, what the team had been through and going 9–3 in that stretch and walking back in there healthy, it was obviously a goal that we had set. What a great job Bruce and the staff and the team did, the way they played and the seven fourth-quarter comebacks and making the playoffs.

Since we had already clinched the playoffs, the big question from the media was, "Are you going to play the guys? Are you going to play the starters?" I was like, "C'mon. Are you really asking me that?" I had been gone for twelve weeks and going through what we went through, fighting your ass off to get healthy and get in remission and I'm going to come back and we're not going to play to win the game? Are you kidding me? I laughed at that. I said from day one that we signed up for 16 games and by God we were going to play to win 16 games, especially this one.

I can remember going through the week and trying to get back to normalcy. It wasn't going to be like flipping a switch and jumping right back into the role. It's like riding a bike. You never forget how to ride a bike, but there was some adjustment there. It was getting up Sunday morning and going to the stadium and going through your routine, then actually walking out there. Avis (Roper, senior director of communications) and those guys were telling me, "Hey, we're going to need to be with you and help you go out there. There are going to be a few reporters and cameras out there." I didn't have any idea what it was going to be like. My legs were weary, to be quite honest with you. Just a bit shaky when you walk out there. It was very humbling.

I was back at work, back on the field, back with the team, and back in the stadium. It was special. I can remember Mr. McNair (Houston owner Robert McNair) and that whole contingent coming over from the Texans. They were so respectful and kind.

Once we got through all of the pregame stuff, we had a game to win. We got past that, said our final words (in the locker room), and came back out and the ball was kicked off. Then it was pretty much back to normal. You kind of get lost in the moment and forget for three hours and five minutes what the hell had just transpired to get back on the field.

We came out like gangbusters. We jumped on 'em and it was 14–6. Then they came back and took the lead (16–14) before Deji Karim housed that kickoff return (101-yard touchdown). I remember the middle of the coverage opened up like the Red Sea, and nobody laid a hand on that kid. He just took off. The closest defender was like 40 yards away. That ignited our sideline, and we never trailed again.

Chuck Pagano celebrated his return to the sideline with fans following the Colts' 28–16 win over the Houston Texans in the final game of the 2012 regular season.

Then to be able to go in there and win that game and the way we won it was amazing, especially the way we finished the game.

(The Colts led, 28–16, and took possession at their own 20-yard line with 9:46 to play. Houston's offense never saw the field again.)

It was a 12-play drive (15 counting three game-ending Andrew Luck kneel-downs), and we ran on 11 of them. We threw one pass. It was crazy. I've seen a lot of stuff in my years, but it's hard to have a nine-minute, forty-six-second drive to get on a knee to win a game. That's classic. I'll never forget it. We needed one more first down to get to the two-minute (warning) and get on the knee. As soon as we got it and called for the victory group to get out there, that's when you start celebrating on the sidelines.

Seems like yesterday. It was awesome. I was hugging the players and hugging BA (Arians). It was classic. It was a pretty special moment.

The Aftermath

The initial euphoria ended when Pagano and his Colts dropped a 24–9 decision to the Ravens in Baltimore in a first-round playoff matchup. But it nonetheless represented an authoritative first step for a franchise that had finished tied with the St. Louis Rams with a league-worst 2–14 record in 2011.

Pagano joined San Francisco's Jim Harbaugh as the only head coaches in NFL history to lead his team to at least 11 wins in each of his first three years. He joined Tony Dungy and Ted Marchibroda as the only coaches in Colts history to take a team to the playoffs in each of his first three seasons. The Colts went a step further in the playoffs each season, capped by a trip to the AFC Championship Game following the 2014 season.

The 2015 season represented yet another hurdle for Pagano and the Colts to clear. They slipped to an 8–8 record and failed to make the playoffs, as Luck missed nine games with injuries and Pagano's job was in jeopardy.

Yet one day after a 30–24 victory over the Tennessee Titans to close the season, owner Jim Irsay signed Pagano to a four-year extension.

"Things have worked out just the way they were supposed to," Pagano said. "There's a plan. I took my hands off the wheel a long time ago. You work hard and do the best you can. That's a credit to everybody in this building and those players first and foremost."

The ultimate goal remains unchanged: bring another Lombardi Trophy to Indianapolis. No one said it was going to be easy, and it hasn't been.

"Sometimes you've got to go through some stuff, go through the fire, to harden yourself to get yourself ready," Pagano said. "It's easy when you're out front and you've got a big lead. But when you're fighting for your life or fighting for this or fighting for that, that's when you really find out about everybody.

"I don't take any days for granted. I'm blessed to be talking to you right now about this. I'm grateful to have the opportunity to continue to build this thing and chase the Holy Grail, if you will, and reach the mountaintop.

"Unbelievable."

CHAPTER 7

DAVID
THORNTON

Linebacker 2002–2005

**October 6, 2003, vs. Tampa Bay Buccaneers
at Raymond James Stadium**

INDIANAPOLIS COLTS 38, TAMPA BAY BUCCANEERS 35 (OT)

The hype machine sprang to life in April, when the NFL released its 2003 schedule. Of the 512 regular-season games on the docket, one seemed to attract the most interest: October 6, Indianapolis Colts versus the Buccaneers in Tampa.

"It will be a big game and a tough game," Tony Dungy said. "They're very tough at home, especially on Monday night."

Nice try, coach.

As much as Dungy tried to downplay Colts versus Bucs, at some level he realized it was a losing proposition. It would mark his first meeting with the team that fired him after the Bucs suffered a second consecutive first-round loss at Philadelphia in the 2001 playoffs. Shortly after being discarded by Tampa Bay, Dungy was named the Colts' head coach.

And let's not forget yet another subplot: October 6 was Dungy's birthday. He'd turn forty-eight the day of the game.

As the game neared, the buildup intensified.

Dungy's Colts were 4–0 and coming off a 55–21 pummeling of New Orleans during which quarterback Peyton Manning passed for 314 yards and a franchise-record six touchdowns. The Bucs, now following the lead of Jon Gruden, were 2–1. They were reigning Super Bowl champions and flashed the league's No. 1-rated defense.

Still, Dungy did his best to approach the Bucs as just the next game on the schedule.

"Our distraction is with Tampa Bay and the fact that they're a good football team and defending champions," he said. "We've got to go down there and obviously play well to win.

"Other than that, there shouldn't be too many distractions. I hope the game doesn't turn into a sideshow with the game itself being a small part of things. The game should be a major part. Playing on Monday night. The defending champions. We're 4–0. That should be the storyline. I think that would be a great storyline but probably won't be."

As their coach talked of making the Bucs simply the next opponent on the schedule, the players understood the magnitude of the game.

"That's Tony," second-year linebacker David Thornton said. "He's never going to make any game bigger than another game. Every game is the biggest game. You treat them all the same, so that's how he approached it.

"But as players and the people around him, we knew and understood the other implications and the other factors surrounding the game. That made it that much more meaningful for us. It was his birthday. It was his first game back in Tampa. It was a Monday night game. It was all of that. He wouldn't come out and say it, but it definitely gave the game a little more spice."

When Dungy walked out of the tunnel several hours before kickoff, he made it a point to re-connect with fans lining the edge of the stands. He chatted and signed autographs. He sought out former players—Derrick Brooks, John Lynch, Ronde Barber, Warren Sapp—and shared emotional embraces.

The game? One for the ages.

Dungy's new team gave him the best present possible—a 38–35 overtime win—but only after trailing his old team, 21–0, at the half, 28–7, after three quarters, and 35–14, with 5:09 remaining. The Colts became the first team in NFL history to win after trailing by 21 points with five minutes to play.

Notes on David Thornton

Joined Colts: Fourth-round draft pick in 2002, 106th overall selection

Jersey No.: 50

Birthdate: November 1, 1978

Height: 6-2

Weight: 230

Games/starts with

Colts: 63/47

Highlights: Finished Colts career with 394 total tackles, including 239 solos. Also had three sacks, three interceptions, and four forced fumbles. Started five of seven playoff games and had team-high 26 tackles in three starts during 2003 postseason. NFL career spanned eight seasons and ended after 2009 season following four years with Tennessee Titans. Walked on at North Carolina and eventually earned a scholarship. Was named team MVP as a senior on a team that included Julius Peppers.

The Game

By David Thornton

That game in particular was probably one of the most memorable game experiences I've ever been a part of in my NFL life. Just the emotion in the locker room after we won. Knowing what we had overcome to get there.

Even the hype leading up to the game was something else. It was *Monday Night Football.* Tampa Bay was the defending champs and a very tough team. It was Tony Dungy's first time back in Tampa since he had left. It was Tony's birthday. There were a lot of reasons for us to be excited about the game. It was the national stage.

The team, the players, we all wanted to go out and play hard for Coach Dungy. He definitely had won the approval of the guys early on, and we always played hard for him. To have the chance to go back and represent him in a strong way, we wanted to do that. There was a lot surrounding that game, believe me.

But anything that could go wrong early went wrong. Early on, we were not playing Colts football. From the turnovers to getting a big play from Mike Doss (an interception of Brad Johnson) and him fumbling and Keenan McCardell picking it up and scoring. It was crazy. It was a disaster. Mike Doss made a great play and a horrible play all on the same play. It was crazy.

Things weren't looking favorably for us. As the game progressed, maybe people who had been watching gave up on us. I just remember the stories the next day how people were shocked to hear that we won the game. Many fans had turned their TVs off when we were down a significant number of points with not much time remaining. They went to bed.

But coach Dungy always stressed to us just to keep our hands on the plow and keep working, keep doing the things we were taught to do. Just have that persistence, find a way to make plays.

We got a key return by Brad Pyatt (90-yard kickoff return to the Bucs' 12-yard line). Then things started going our way. Marvin (Harrison) got a touchdown (28 yards) during our surge. Troy Walters had a couple of big third-down conversions for us. It just started turning around.

We never gave up hope. Honestly, I always was taught to play hard for 60 minutes. Despite the scoreboard, we kept playing hard. I suppose the human element does kick in at some point, but me personally and the linebackers, we all wanted to keep playing hard.

Defensively, we had to find ways to get off the field to get the ball back to our offense. We knew what our offense could do, so we had to come up with some crucial stops down the stretch.

When we got to overtime, you could feel on the sidelines the confidence go to another level. It was, "Hey, this is our game. This is *our* game. We're not going to lose." The fact we made it to overtime was almost a sense of relief. *Man, now we've got it.*

Fans had trouble believing it the next day, but linebacker David Thornton and the Colts rallied from a 35–14 deficit with less than five minutes to play to post a 38–35 overtime victory.

(Placekicker Mike Vanderjagt converted the game-winning 29-yard field goal with 3:47 remaining in overtime, but only after a seldom-called "leaping" penalty was called on Bucs' defensive end Simeon Rice that nullified Vanderjagt's errant 40-yard attempt.)

I remember the kick and the questionable call the referee made. Leaping or whatever it was. But I felt at that time we were destined to win that game. That penalty led to Vanderjagt getting another chance, and he made it. (It ricocheted off the right upright.) He grazed it, but it went in. It put the icing on the cake for how that game unfolded, to end in that fashion.

The Aftermath

What remained of the sellout Raymond James Stadium crowd on what actually was the early morning of October 7 was in shock. They had just witnessed one of the greatest comebacks—or collapses—in NFL history.

Thornton contributed a team-high 15 tackles, including 10 solos.

"It was a total team effort," he said. "It was one of my better games, but honestly I don't remember that part of it. I don't remember it being a great performance by me at all. I was just trying to make a contribution, like every other player.

"I just remember how exhausted and drained we were as a team when the game was over. Oh, my goodness. The joy we had in the locker room as a team was unbelievable. The smiles. The emotions. It was sheer happiness. It was family, camaraderie. We knew we had done something special. We didn't know how the game would fall in history, but we knew that was a special game with a special ending.

"We were so excited and so happy for Coach Dungy to be able to pull off that win for our leader. It meant a lot to everyone. It was a remarkable experience, it really was."

To this day, Thornton finds it difficult to grasp the enormity of the achievement.

"It was incredible," he said. "Down 21 points with under five minutes to play. Just thinking about that is a little mind-blowing. But that's the nature of the game.

"There are so many life lessons you can take from football. One of the most important is never to give up. The impossible can be possible with belief, confidence, staying with the process, and just really staying determined.

"There are so many positive messages you can take from a game like that."

CHAPTER 8

EDGERRIN JAMES

Running back 1999–2005
October 31, 1999, vs. Dallas Cowboys at RCA Dome
INDIANAPOLIS COLTS 34, DALLAS COWBOYS 24

Edgerrin James's introduction to Indianapolis, his home away from home for the next seven years, began with one serious issue: he wasn't the "other running back."

James was African-American and proudly wore dreadlocks, but he wasn't Ricky Williams.

As the 1999 NFL draft approached, it was imperative general manager Bill Polian find a replacement for Marshall Faulk, the Colts' three-time Pro Bowl running back he traded to the St. Louis Rams to avoid a contract dispute. All signs pointed toward that replacement being Williams, Texas's Heisman Trophy-winning running back. A franchise that seldom shared its pre-draft intentions actually made Williams available when it had him in for a visit.

At the earlier NFL Scouting Combine, which is held in Indianapolis, reporters gathered around James at the players' hotel, mistaking him for Williams. Again, he fit the description: an African-American running back with dreads. Oops.

And when it came time for Polian to invest the fourth overall selection in the draft, most expected it to deliver Ricky Williams to the roster.

Notes on Edgerrin James

Joined Colts:	No. 4 overall pick in 1999 draft
Jersey No.:	32
Birthdate:	August 1, 1978
Height:	6-0
Weight:	220
Games/starts with Colts:	96/96
Highlights:	Set franchise records 9,226 rushing yards and 2,188 attempts. Holds single-season team record 1,709 yards (2000) and single-game mark with 219 yards (at Seattle in 2000). Also posted the only other 200-yard game in Colts history with 204 yards a Chicago in 2004. Became fifth player to lead the NFL in rushing in his first two seasons (1,553 yards in 1999, 1,709 in 2000) and the first since Eric Dickerson in 1983–84. Joined Dickerson, Barry Sanders, and Walter Payton as the only players in league history to rush for at least 1,500 yards four times. Named to the first team of the All-Decade Team of the 2000s. Named to four Pro Bowls and was one of fifteen modern-day finalists for the Pro Football Hall of Fame's Class of 2016. Ranks No. 11 in NFL history with 12,246 rushing yards and No. 13 with 15,610 total yards from scrimmage.

Nope. It was Edgerrin James, an all-purpose talent who left the University of Miami a year early.

"I was on the phone to the (Colts) coaches, and they said they were going to take me with the fourth pick," James said. "I was like, 'I'll believe it when I see it.' I wanted to see it come across the TV.

"You hear all these draft-day stories and I didn't want to get my hopes high. I knew wherever I went I'd be happy."

Fans, though, weren't the least bit happy. At a team-sponsored draft party, they booed when his name flashed across the screen. Polian joked he had one of his trusted assistants start his car the night of the draft, fearing it might have been tampered with.

James wasn't the popular choice but proved to be the right one.

"We thought he was the best football player," owner Jim Irsay said.

James considered a future of taking handoffs from Manning and smiled.

"Me and Peyton are starting off young," he said. "We have a lot of time to work to where everything gets to be second nature.

"There are a lot of good combos. Like (Dallas running back) Emmitt (Smith) and (quarterback) Troy Aikman or (Denver's) John Elway and Terrell Davis. That's what I foresee here."

The emergence of James, Manning, and wide receiver Marvin Harrison as legitimate "Triplets" soon rivaled that of Dallas's Troy Aikman, Emmitt Smith, and Michael Irvin. Each set was on display on October 31, 1999, in the RCA Dome.

The Game

By Edgerrin James

I remember the Cowboys came in with Deion Sanders and Aikman and Smith and all those guys. When you grew up in Immokalee and the Fort Myers area and the 239 (area code), you always looked to be out there with Deion. You always wanted to play with Deion. Then you've got Emmitt. You've got Michael Irvin, although I think he was hurt at the time. You've got Aikman. They were *the* team back then.

That was a game that really sticks out. It was kind of like a changing of the guard.

I know before the game everybody was talking about them. I can remember during warm-ups us always looking down, trying to check out what they're doing. That was something that was unusual. We're usually just focusing on ourselves. But that one game, everybody just sort of checked them out, how they went about their business.

We knew we had something good—me and Marv and Peyton—but they had been doing it for so long. Then everybody starts making the comparison. That kind of raised your awareness of the whole situation. You know, these guys had accomplished so much. They had gone out there and done it year in and year out. That's what we wanted to do. It's all about doing it over and over again.

They had done what we wanted to do. They were the blueprint.

(James out-rushed Smith 117–93. Manning passed for 313 yards and one touchdown, while Aikman had 159 yards and no touchdowns. Harrison finished with 85 yards, including a 40-yard touchdown when he beat Sanders's coverage.)

Marv was really getting good. I had a good game. We all went out there and played. We just wanted to play well. When we did that, we figured the end result would always take care of itself. It was always the same. If everybody goes out and does what he's supposed to do, the game will take care of itself. You never got hung up trying to go against this guy or that guy. It's just a matter of being out there and doing what you've prepared all week to do.

That was one of those games where you played the game, then you walked to the sideline and actually watched (Dallas's offense) while our

Running back Edgerrin James (32) enjoyed being part of the Colts' "Triplets" along with quarterback Peyton Manning (18) and receiver Marvin Harrison (88).

defense was on the field. You didn't normally do that. You went to the sideline and got ready for the next time you had to go out. But they were special. You knew that.

We ended up winning the game, then I looked for Deion. He was Deion, you know what I'm talking about? He was legendary in our area (Sanders was from Fort Myers), so to be out there on the field with him was something special. Just to be on the same field with him while he's still playing? Shoot. It didn't get any better than that. And trust me, Deion was still good.

We did what we were supposed to do and everybody came together. We tried to duplicate (Dallas). The beauty of it is we all remained friends to this day. We all stay in touch with one another. Whenever Marv comes down (to Florida), we hang out. We talk all the time. I check in with Peyton from time to time.

That's what made the whole thing so special. We weren't just teammates who played, then once you leave the locker room you never saw one another again. We actually stay in touch. If Peyton changes his phone number, he'll text me, "Hey, this is my new number." Same with Marv. We all do that.

The Aftermath

Indianapolis's Triplets were dissolved after 2005, James's seventh season with the team that brought him into the NFL. The team balked at reinvesting in a player, more specifically a player at a position that takes a heavy toll on the body, who would turn twenty-eight prior to the start of the '06 season. Moreover, Polian saw a running back who had logged 2,188 rushing attempts in those seven seasons.

The Colts decided it was time to move on from a franchise cornerstone. James had won two NFL rushing titles, been selected to four Pro Bowls, and set all-time franchise records with 9,226 rushing yards and 12,065 total yards from scrimmage (since surpassed by Harrison).

James disagreed but by and large kept things civil.

"I did my part. That's the way I looked at it," he said. "I did whatever I could and I made a difference.

"When I was going to the team (in '99), people were saying, 'Man, you're going to a 3–13 team.' My first year, we were 13–3. I never had a losing season there when I played all the time."

He suffered a season-ending knee injury in sixth game of the '01 season at Kansas City, and the Colts spiraled to a 6–10 record. In his six full seasons, the team went 71–25.

"At the end of the day, I can say I did my part, I did what they asked me to do," James said. "Look at the difference when I'm there and when I'm not there. There's nothing you can do to knock my game."

James insisted he was "cool" with the Colts' decision to not re-sign him.

"I have no hard feelings toward anybody," he said. "I've had fun there. Mr. Irsay (owner Jim) is cool. I don't know if there is a better owner to play for."

The feelings were mutual. Even though James no longer was around, Irsay made certain he received a diamond-studded championship ring from the Colts' Super Bowl XLI win over the Chicago Bears.

James would play four more seasons, including three with the Arizona Cardinals after relocating from Indianapolis. He rushed for at least 1,000 yards in his first two seasons with the Cardinals and helped them reach Super Bowl XLIII after the 2008 season.

James retired after spending the 2009 season with the Seattle Seahawks.

A career that began with an ultra-confident rookie out of the University of Miami leading the NFL in rushing as a rookie ended with James ranking among the best in league history.

He ranks No. 11 in NFL history with 12,246 rushing yards and No. 13 with 15,610 total yards from scrimmage. He also was named one of fifteen modern-day finalists for the Pro Football Hall of Fame's Class of 2016, although he fell short of being enshrined in his second year of eligibility.

"It was always important for me to leave a lasting impression on everybody," James said. "I wanted people to say, 'He did it the right way. He didn't compromise who he was. He didn't compromise where he was from. He did things his way, but it also was the right way.'"

CHAPTER 9

AARON BAILEY

Wide receiver 1994–98

January 14, 1996, vs. Pittsburgh Steelers at Three Rivers Stadium

1995 AFC Championship Game

PITTSBURGH STEELERS 20, INDIANAPOLIS COLTS 16

No one saw it coming. In fact, one of the most unlikely playoff runs in NFL history and a Hail Mary that nearly was answered in the end zone at Three Rivers Stadium almost didn't materialize.

Three weeks before Jim Harbaugh's spiral sliced through the unseasonably warm air in Pittsburgh and tried to find its way to Aaron Bailey's hands amid a mass of humanity, the Indianapolis Colts were on the verge of being eliminated from the 1995 postseason picture altogether. They needed a victory in their regular-season finale at home against New England to finish 9–7 and secure a wild-card playoff berth.

The Colts trailed, 7–0, at the half, but so what? This was a bunch that refused to lose while overcoming 21-point third-quarter road deficits against the Miami Dolphins and New York Jets. With everything on the line against the Patriots, they gathered themselves and followed Captain Comeback—the nickname given to Harbaugh during the frenetic '95 season—to a 10–7 win.

They were in the playoffs for just the second time since their relocation to Indianapolis in 1984 and the first time since '87.

It was the beginning of what would be a wild ride.

Despite being double-digit road underdogs, the Colts upset San Diego, 35–20, and stunned the Kansas City Chiefs, 10–7.

"It was probably one of the best times in my playing career," Bailey said. "Every day, going to practice was a great experience. There was a buzz going on around the city. You could sense the excitement when you were out in the community. I'll never forget the reception we received at the airport after we beat the Kansas City Chiefs.

Notes on Aaron Bailey

Joined Colts:	Undrafted free agent in 1994
Jersey No.:	80
Birthdate:	October 24, 1971
Height:	5-10
Weight:	185
Games/starts with Colts:	64/9
Highlights:	Collected 67 receptions for 1,040 yards and six touchdowns during five-year career with Colts. Had best season in 1995 with 21 receptions, 379 yards, and three TDs. Major contributor on special teams. Returned 20 punts for 195 yards and a 9.8 average, and returned 153 kickoffs for 3,501 yards (22.9 average) with a club-record-tying two touchdowns. Kickoff returns rank No. 3 in franchise history, while kickoff return yards rank No. 2.

"Everyone kept counting us out, but we kept finding ways to win. We got on a roll."

Then, it was on to the AFC Championship game in Pittsburgh.

The Game

By Aaron Bailey

I don't think about that game until someone brings it up, to be honest with you. Playing in the NFL is like another lifetime ago. When the playoffs roll around, you find yourself talking about it, because it was a big sports moment and a big part of your life.

It's hard to describe the buzz that was in our locker room and the buzz that was in the city. Nobody had given us a chance (against the Steelers), but we expected to go there and win, the same way we did going into San Diego and going into Kansas City. There was the same thought process going into Pittsburgh. Nothing changed. We were a hot team and we knew it.

There was no doubt in my mind we were going to find a way to win, we were going to make a play. But you see all the things that happened . . . Slash (Kordell Stewart) stepping out of bounds (on a touchdown catch), crucial fourth-down plays, Lamont (Warren) getting tripped up on a counter play where their guy wasn't supposed to blitz off the edge, the (potential interception) going off Quentin Coryatt's chest, a slant-and-go against Ashley Ambrose where Ernie Mills made a big play.

The Lamont play is the one that really sticks out.

(The Colts led, 16–13, and faced a 3rd-and-1 at their own 31-yard line with three minutes to play. A first down would virtually seal a stunning upset.)

He picks that up and the game's over. When we called that play, I said, "Game's over." I told (teammate) Bobby Olive, who's my best friend to this day, "Bobby, game's over. We're going to the Super Bowl." And Lamont got tripped up. (Steelers defensive back Willie Williams) wasn't supposed to be there (for the tackle).

Things like that make you sick to your stomach. You're right there. You do the perfect thing at the perfect time and it doesn't go your way. It was ours for the taking. Give (the Steelers) credit, but there were so many perfect things that went their way during the game, so many perfect plays. All along, I'm thinking something was going to break for us.

(The Colts trailed, 20-16, with 1:34 to play and started the final drive at their own 16-yard line.)

On that last drive, our thought process was to get down there and score. We had been in that situation before, so there wasn't any panic in our mind. We were down, 24–3, against Miami earlier in the season and came back and won in overtime. There was never any panic in our mind as we were driving the ball down the field. It was like, "OK, here we go again."

It got to the point where we were close enough to run the Hail Mary. (Third-and-1 at the Steelers, 29-yard line with five seconds remaining.)

We thought we were going to make it happen. Never in our minds did we have any doubt. We were just going to go out there and execute the play. It was just our Hail Mary play. We were in our "trips" formation. I was in the middle on the right side (with Brian Stablein and Floyd Turner). The only thing I was thinking was, "Jim, just leave it in bounds. Give us a shot." Which he did. He gave us a great throw.

Brian Stablein had the highest vertical on the team and probably one of the highest in the NFL. He was supposed to be the tip guy. Floyd (Turner) and I were supposed to be the catchers. For whatever reason, I just took off and ran down field. You're basically just trying to get into position to make the play. But I found myself in a position where, "Wait a minute, the ball's coming down and it's coming down right toward me."

In a matter of seconds, the roles have changed. As you see the ball start to come down, you start to feel guys grabbing your arms, pulling you down. They're grabbing, pulling, holding onto your arms. I'm trying to shake my left arm free. I'm trying to shake them off my right arm. Someone's trying to hold me. There's a whole lot of jostling going on down there.

Then you jump up. You've got a couple of big corners in there and a couple of corners my size and a lot of guys surrounding you. You just go up and try your best to make the attempt to get the catch.

You see a lot of articles that say, "He dropped the ball." No. I don't think I had a drop the whole season. I was thinking, "That's not right. If I had gotten my hands on it, I would have caught it. Are you kidding me?"

You slow things down to super-super slow motion, you might see the ball land on my stomach for a few seconds. All the while in real speed you've got whiplash because your head hits the turf so hard. You darn near get a concussion. You don't know anything about a ball laying on your stomach or even touching your stomach.

Everything happened in slow motion as Colts' receiver Aaron Bailey (white jersey) attempted to control Jim Harbaugh's Hail Mary pass on the final play of the 1995 AFC Championship Game in Pittsburgh.

I know I gave it my best shot and I'm at peace with it. I saw the ball. I saw it, I saw it, I saw it. It's one of those things where you're almost in a dream and you just can't reach something. It's right there and you reach for it, but you just can't reach it. You ever have those dreams where something's right in front of you, but you just can't grab it? You can't grab it, you can't grab it, you can't grab it. That's what that was like.

It was one of things where "It's right here. Why can't I get to it?"

(While Bailey was on the ground, Turner and Stablein raised their hands to signal a catch and a touchdown.)

That's what you do. That's how you're taught. The ball was trapped and was in the bottom of the pile and I had a decision to make. I was like, "Shoot, flash that way. We need this. This is our shot." You grab the ball and put it up in the air. But the ref made the call and the game was over.

Once the ref was waving it off, that's when reality set in that we actually lost.

The Aftermath

The encore lacked the electricity of the original but was successful nonetheless. After reaching the AFC title game in '95, the Colts again posted a 9–7 record in '96. They advanced to the playoffs in consecutive seasons for the first time since 1976–77.

"We had a great, great run," Bailey said. "We'll all be connected with one another one way or the other. We will all have a special bond with one another. We'll all be connected to (the '95 AFC title game) and everything we accomplished.

"That brought us together and we started something we can be proud of . . . seeing the success the Colts are having now, seeing the Colts win the Super Bowl (after the 2006 season), seeing everything that has happened.

"Just talking about it now is kind of bringing a tear to my eyes. It was that special."

CHAPTER 10

ERIC DICKERSON

Running back 1987–1991
October 31, 1988, vs. Denver Broncos at Hoosier Dome
INDIANAPOLIS COLTS 55, DENVER BRONCOS 23

Eric Dickerson and the Colts resided at opposite ends of the NFL landscape in the mid-1980s, and that had nothing to do with Los Angeles and Indianapolis being separated by nearly 2,000 miles.

Dickerson was the big-time player in the big-time market with the big-time résumé. As a Los Angeles Rams running back in 1983, he led the league in rushing with a rookie-record 1,808 yards. For an encore, Dickerson again led the NFL in rushing, this time with 2,105 yards, which eclipsed O. J. Simpson's single-season mark.

While Dickerson was making his mark on the West Coast, the Colts were simply trying to gain a foothold in the Midwest. Their initial steps in the NFL after relocating to Indianapolis from Baltimore in 1984 included 4–12, 5–11, and 3–13 records. Prior to moving, the Colts had endured six consecutive losing seasons and a combined 26–62–1 record.

Everything changed on October 31, 1987.

The Rams had grown weary of Dickerson's stubborn demands for a new contract. He held out for more than a month in '85 and missed the first two games of the season.

"No one player is bigger than the team," Rams coach John Robinson said. "When the contract begins to affect on-the-field activities, it's time to make a move."

That move was to Indianapolis in what remains one of the biggest trades in NFL history. It involved the Rams, Colts, and Buffalo Bills and consisted of ten moving parts. Most notably, it sent Dickerson to Indianapolis and Cornelius Bennett, the Colts' 1987 first-round draft pick who was holding out, to Buffalo.

"I knew they were trying to send me to Siberia to punish me. Literally they were," he said. "And they did, in a sense.

"Honestly, I told them I wanted to go to the Redskins. I knew that wasn't going to happen. Then I went to Indy."

The Colts satisfied Dickerson's contract demands with a four-year, $5.6 million contract, but he insisted the only reason he agreed to report and consummate the blockbuster trade was the presence of coach Ron Meyer. Meyer was Dickerson's coach at Southern Methodist University.

"If they had traded me and Ron hadn't been there, I probably wouldn't have gone," Dickerson said. "It would have been, 'Nope, I'm not going.'

"Ron had been my college coach and I trusted him. In college, my mom loved him. To the day she died, she always trusted him. And I trusted him. Ron Meyer was the reason I came to Indy.

"I knew absolutely nothing about Indy. I had an uncle who lived there. Other than that, I knew nothing about Indy. I didn't know my friend Harvey Armstrong played there and we went to college together."

Dickerson gave the Colts instant credibility in NFL circles, and a game-breaking star on the field. He rushed for 1,011 yards and five touchdowns in nine games in his first season, then everyone braced for more in '88.

Dickerson didn't disappoint. In his first full season with the Colts, he captured his third league rushing title in four years with a franchise-record 1,659 yards. He also led the league with 388 rushing attempts and 2,036 yards from scrimmage.

The brightest moment occurred on the one-year anniversary of the trade that reshaped Dickerson's career and gave the Colts a national identity. Halloween 1988 won't soon be forgotten.

Notes on Eric Dickerson

Joined Colts:	Trade in 1987 involving Los Angeles Rams and Buffalo Bills
Jersey No.:	29
Birthdate:	September 2, 1960
Height:	6-3
Weight:	220
Games/starts with Colts:	61/55
Highlights:	Acquired in one of the biggest trades in NFL history. The deal included the Rams and Bills, and consisted of ten players or draft picks. Appeared in 61 games with the Colts, and ranks No. 4 all-time in rushing yards (5,194) and No. 9 in yards from scrimmage (6,276). In his first full season with the team in 1988, led the NFL in rushing (1,659 yards) and yards from scrimmage (2,036). Each was a franchise single-season record. A five-time first-team All-Pro and inducted into the Pro Football Hall of Fame in 1999. Set NFL rookie rushing record with 1,808 yards in 1983 and set league single-season rushing record with 2,105 yards in '84. Only player in league history with three seasons of at least 1,800 rushing yards. Ranks No. 7 in league history with 13,259 yards, No. 9 with 2,996 rushing attempts, and tied for No. 13 with 90 rushing touchdowns. Originally was taken with the second overall pick in the 1983 draft by the Los Angeles Rams. Appeared in 146 games with the Rams, Colts, Oakland Raiders, and Atlanta Falcons.

On ABC's *Monday Night Football* stage, the Colts bolted to a 45–10 halftime lead en route to a 55–23 demolition of the Denver Broncos. Dickerson rushed 21 times for 159 yards and four touchdowns.

Not impressed? Consider he was pulled early in the third quarter after three carries on the opening possession netted 35 yards.

The Game

By Eric Dickerson

It was so long ago, but it was a great game. It was a great game for us as a team and for the city. I think it was the first Monday Night game they had (it was the second). It was one of those electrifying nights. Everything went right that night. I mean *everything* went right.

I had a really, really good game in the first half (18 carries, 124 yards, four TDs), then they took me out early in the third quarter. I begged them to keep me in. Ron (Meyer) was like, "No." I was like, "Really?" I told him, "Days like this aren't going to come around that often. Leave me in." But they wouldn't put me back in. I understand from a coach's point of view, I really do. But I wanted to stay in. I know how it goes.

I knew we were going to have a good game even during warm-ups. I could feel it. First of all, we knew (Denver's) defense was having a hard time stopping the run. There were some plays we had put in specifically for that game. We knew they would work. I felt injury-free, and that's another thing. When you don't have any injuries bothering you, you feel like the sky's the limit. It was all good.

Every time I touched the ball, I felt like I could score a touchdown.

(Dickerson's first 15 rushing attempts included touchdown runs of 12, 11, 1, and 41 yards.)

You feel fast. You feel light. Every cut you make is right. Everything just works. Seriously, it was one of those games where everything went our way. You hear people talk about it being "one of those nights," well, that's exactly what it was. Believe me, they come along rarely, they really do. It can happen against a good team. It can happen against a bad team.

When you feel it, it's like there's nothing going to stop you. That's how it works. Every time I got the ball, I expected something good to happen. And it did.

Like I said, things worked from the start. I think I had three touchdowns in the first quarter. I think I had four all day. I know I had 159 (yards). I kind of lost count of the touchdowns.

The star of the Colts' appearance on Monday Night Football in 1988 was running back Eric Dickerson. He was the catalyst of the 55–23 blowout with 159 yards and four touchdowns.

What made it special was there were only Monday Night games at the time—they weren't playing on Thursday night—and we knew everybody was watching. That was it. Everybody watched *Monday Night Football*.

I only wish Ron had left me in the game. Yeah, I wanted to stay in. I was on pace to get 2,000 yards again. I knew that, and that's something you strive for as a running back.

If Ron had left me in, oh man, I think I could have had 300-plus yards that night. The way the game was going, I believe I would have had one of those 60- or 70-yarders. But, hey, it wasn't meant to happen. That's how it goes.

After the game, you knew we had done something special, something that doesn't come along very often.

The Aftermath

The high-profile marriage consummated on October 31, 1987, lasted less than four-and-a-half years. Like the Rams, the Colts lost patience with Dickerson's disruptive ways.

After a couple of suspensions and with Dickerson's availability and productivity limited by injuries and his reluctance to run behind what he considered to be a substandard offensive line, the Colts traded him to the Oakland Raiders on April 26, 1992. It was hardly a blockbuster deal. The Raiders sent the Colts fourth- and eighth-round draft picks.

Indianapolis, Dickerson said, "was just part of my career. It was OK at first. I did some things that I hate happened. There were some things that got out of hand. I always say, 'It is what it is.'

"Any time you put on a uniform in the National Football League, it's a blessing. You're not going to play that long. I'm happy I was in a Colts uniform. It had a lot of history behind it, in Indianapolis and in Baltimore."

CHAPTER 11

ADAM VINATIERI

Placekicker 2006–present

January 13, 2007, vs. Baltimore Ravens at M&T Bank Stadium

2006 AFC Divisional Playoffs

INDIANAPOLIS COLTS 15, BALTIMORE RAVENS 6

The transition from bold to subdued came following an errant field-goal attempt that remains one of the most notorious plays in Colts' history.

Mike Vanderjagt's 46-yard attempt in the closing seconds of a 2005 AFC divisional playoff loss to the Pittsburgh Steelers sailed wide right, sealed an excruciating 21–18 loss, and essentially ended his record-setting eight-year career with the team.

It had always been an uneasy relationship that tested management's tolerance for brashness from a player at a position known more for kicking than conversation.

It ended in February 2006, when team president Bill Polian, more than tired of his kicker's flamboyant persona and inability to deliver in the clutch against the Steelers and the Miami Dolphins in a 2000 overtime playoff loss, decided not to re-sign the franchise's all-time scoring leader.

Moving on from Vanderjagt was necessary, but it left a cavernous hole.

"It's one thing to say (a player) shouldn't be back," said coach Tony Dungy. "You have to get people that are better. That's what we always are going to try to do.

"We're not going to get rid of people unless we have good alternatives."

A good alternative? As it turned out, the Colts found arguably the best.

On March 22, 2006, Adam Vinatieri relocated from New England to Indianapolis.

"This is a tremendous acquisition for the team and it was smartly done," owner Jim Irsay said. "You know you're going to have some close, tough ballgames and a great kicker can make a difference between 12–4 and 10–6."

More important, and as the Colts soon would discover, a great kicker could make the difference in advancing deep in the playoffs, or going home early and wondering what might have been.

Exhibit A: Colts 15, Baltimore Ravens 6 in a 2006 divisional playoff game. More accurately, it was Vinatieri 15, Ravens 6.

Notes on Adam Vinatieri

Joined Colts:	Signed as a free agent in March 2006
Jersey No.:	4
Birthdate:	December 28, 1972
Height:	6-0
Weight:	206
Games/starts with Colts:	146/0
Highlights:	Holds franchise regular-season records with 1,095 points, 240 made field goals, and 277 field-goal attempts. Has converted eight game-winning field goals in the final minute of regulation or overtime with the Colts, and 26 in his 20-year career. Holds team postseason records with 117 points, 30 made field goals, and 34 field-goal attempts. Provided all of the scoring in the Colts' 15-6 victory over the Baltimore Ravens in a 2006 AFC divisional round playoff game. In 2015, was the NFL's oldest player (age forty-three). The only player in NFL history to play at least 10 seasons with two different teams (10 each with Colts and New England Patriots) and the only one to score at least 1,000 points for two teams (1,095 with the Colts, 1,158 with the Patriots). The 2,253 career points rank No. 3 in NFL history. Converted a 48-yard field goal as time expired to give New England a 20–17 win over the St. Louis Rams in Super Bowl XXXVI and kicked a 41-yarder with four seconds remaining that lifted the Patriots to a 32–29 win over Carolina in Super Bowl XXXVIII. Holds NFL postseason records for points (234), made field goals (56), field-goal attempts (68), and PATs (66). He ranks second with 30 games played.

The Game

By Adam Vinatieri

You know every point probably is going to matter. I try to approach every game that way. The games that you think are going to go one way, they go a different way. Very seldom are you right. One thing about playoff games you're generally right about is they're going to be close games, and normally they come down to the last two minutes. You have to be on your stuff. You have to be on top of your game every second.

So your mind-set has to be—for everybody, not just myself—be on your stuff. You have to be on top of your game every second. Usually in the playoffs, the mistake a team makes is the one that costs them the win.

Tony Dungy used to say more games are lost than won, and I totally agree with that one hundred percent. The teams that can just kind of stay focused and just do their job and stay in it without getting too high are the ones that succeed in the end.

We were held to two field goals in the first quarter against the Ravens, and that just told us what everybody knew. Points were going to be hard to come by. We knew that. I think (the Ravens) had one of the best, if not the best, defenses in the league at the time. Every year they had a great defense. It was Ray Lewis and Terrell Suggs and all those studs.

We had a darned good offense that was scoring a ton of points, but when you go up against a good defense, points are at a premium every single time you step on the field.

I remember how I felt after I hit the 51-yarder in the second quarter. Like I said, we knew how difficult it was going to be scoring. It just kissed the top of the crossbar. Just enough. Anytime you kick a 50-yard field goal, you're doing something.

(The Colts led 12–6 with 7:39 remaining.)

We had a nice, long (seven-minute) drive. We ate up a lot of clock. That was pretty impressive against that defense.

For me, I look at how many first downs do we need (to get in position for a field goal)? Do we need two, three first downs? But sometimes a 35-yard pass is like getting three first downs all at once. Usually when we get close to midfield, I start getting ready. That's not to say I'm not staying

The Colts' 15–6 win at Baltimore in the 2006 playoffs was delivered by the right foot of placekicker Adam Vinatieri.

in it all the time, because you never know what might happen. It's when we get to midfield, maybe our 40-yard line. Our offense was explosive enough that we could get chunk plays at a time, quickly.

My thought at the end of that is we were up, 12–6, going into that last field goal. There were something like 30 seconds left. I'm thinking, "This one puts the game away." You're up nine. I remember thinking if we make this one, we win the game. Period. It was nice when that one went through. I remember Tony (Dungy) on the sideline. Everybody made a comment about him (mouthing the word *money*). That was cool.

In playoff games, you calm down and get in your groove. I don't really hear much. I don't know how it happens or why it happens, but everything seems to slow down. It really does. I've had players on other teams jawing at me, saying this and saying that. They think they can get to me. I try to keep my head down and do my job.

The reason they brought me in that year was for games like that. Regular season is what it is. But the reason you go after certain guys is to do well in the postseason.

I walked out of that game thinking, "OK, that's why you're here."

There are a lot of postseason games that come down to a play here or a play there. It's the teams that can execute under the pressure times that are successful, that win championships. That was a hard game. They couldn't get in the end zone, either. Our defense played unbelievable that day. The whole playoff run, our defense was just awesome. Statistically, our defense and our special teams were the reason we continued to advance on, one hundred percent.

The Aftermath

Vinatieri earned his reputation as the best clutch kicker in NFL history during his 10-year stint with the New England Patriots, although his 177-game stats including the playoffs hardly attest to that: 289 of 355, 81.4 percent.

When it mattered and when legacies were formed, he was, to use Dungy's description, money.

Foremost among his 26 career game-winning kicks in the final minute of the fourth quarter or in overtime were a 48-yarder as time expired that gave the Patriots a 20–17 win over the St. Louis Rams in Super Bowl

XXXVI and a 41-yarder with four seconds remaining that produced New England's 32–29 win over Carolina in Super Bowl XXXVIII.

To this day, Vinatieri is most proud of his performance in a 2001 AFC divisional round matchup with the Oakland Raiders in frigid Foxboro Stadium. He pounded a 45-yard field goal through a snowstorm with 27 seconds to play that sent the game into overtime, then tacked on a 23-yarder in overtime to produce the 16–13 victory.

Two games later, Vinatieri KO'd the Rams with his right leg on the NFL's grandest stage.

Vinatieri's relocation to Indianapolis did nothing to tarnish his reputation. His 5-for-5 outing against the Ravens was the second step on an impeccable path to Super Bowl XLI, which saw the Colts handle the Chicago Bears, 29–17. He converted 14 of 15 attempts, including 12 straight at one point.

In seven playoff appearances with the Colts, Vinatieri knocked down 30 of 34 field-goal attempts (88.2 percent) in 13 games.

He ranks second in NFL postseason history with 30 appearances—one more than Jerry Rice, one fewer than Tom Brady–and has a record 234 points. The scoring split: 117 points with the Patriots, 117 with the Colts. His 68 attempts and 56 made field goals also are records.

Money.

"I'm not one hundred percent in the postseason by any means," Vinatieri said. "I've missed some that are tough to swallow. But you hope you can focus in and do your job. We always talk about doing your job. You don't have to do anybody else's. Just do your job and do it well.

"You do everything all season long to have the opportunity to play in the postseason. You get remembered for what happens in the postseason. Everybody realizes that."

CHAPTER 12

ANTOINE BETHEA

Safety 2006–2013
January 6, 2007, vs. Kansas City Chiefs at RCA Dome
2006 AFC Wild Card Playoffs
INDIANAPOLIS COLTS 23, KANSAS CITY CHIEFS 8

A season that opened with nine consecutive wins teetered on the brink. As the 2006 stretch run approached, there were two losses in three games, then a trip to Jacksonville that shook the Indianapolis Colts to their core.

It's remembered not so much for the final score—Jaguars 44, Colts 17—as for the manner with which it was achieved. Jacksonville exhausted its available running backs while bludgeoning the Colts' defense with 375 rushing yards.

Three. Hundred. Seventy. Five. It remains the most rushing yards allowed in franchise history and is tied for the third-most yielded in an NFL regular-season game since the 1970 merger.

"That Jacksonville game was ugly," said Antoine Bethea, a rookie safety at the time. "Fred Taylor and (Maurice) Jones-Drew ran all over us."

It didn't stop with those two. Jones-Drew rushed 15 times for 166 yards, and Taylor needed only nine carries to pile up 131 yards. But No. 3 running back Alvin Pearman tacked on 71 yards on 13 attempts.

The joke at the time was the Jaguars would have piled up a heftier rushing total, but the end zone kept getting in the way. They rushed for four touchdowns, and three covered 18, 21, and 48 yards.

Despite the inglorious performance, the Colts regrouped. Owner Jim Irsay credited the steady hand of coach Tony Dungy, who was selected to the Pro Football Hall of Fame in February 2016.

"Coming out of Jacksonville, I'm telling you there is only a Hall of Fame coach—only a Hall of Fame coach—that could bring that team together to go through the playoffs, stop the run against teams that run the ball like Kansas City," he said. "There is no question that Tony Dungy, to bring us to the Super Bowl victory in '06, he is the individual that believed."

The players listened to their leader. They also received a major boost with the return of difference-making safety Bob Sanders, who had missed 12 of the final 14 games of the regular season with a knee injury, and linebacker Rob Morris, whose playing time had been greatly reduced.

"At the end of the day, we knew we had the type of players to be a good defense," Bethea said. "Something just clicked. It clicked at the right time.

"It was a great, great feeling during that playoff run. A great feeling."

That feeling peaked on February 4, 2007, when the Colts won their first world championship in three decades with a 29–17 victory over the Chicago Bears in Super Bowl XLI.

But its genesis was the first-round playoff game against the Kansas City Chiefs and running back Larry Johnson, who set a franchise record with 1,789 yards during the regular season.

Notes on Antoine Bethea

Joined Colts:	Sixth-round pick in 2006, 207th overall selection.
Jersey No.:	41
Birthdate:	July 27, 1984
Height:	5-11
Weight:	206
Games/starts with Colts:	123/123
Highlights:	One of the Colts' better draft acquisitions. Inserted into the starting lineup as a rookie in '06 and would start all 16 regular-season games in six of eight seasons with the team. Finished career in Indianapolis in 2013 with a streak of 96 consecutive starts, which was the longest active streak in the NFL by a safety. Was selected to the Pro Bowl after the 2007 and '09 seasons. Selected by his teammates as recipient of the Ed Block Courage award in 2012 and the team's "NFL Man of the Year" candidate. Had 935 tackles and 14 interceptions in 123-game Indianapolis career. Signed with the San Francisco 49ers as an unrestricted free agent after the 2013 season. Started 23 games with 49ers and registered 129 tackles and four interceptions through 2015.

The Game
By Antoine Bethea

My first playoff game was against the Kansas City Chiefs. Maybe not a lot of people remember that game, but it stands out to me for a lot of reasons. That year, we weren't really great against the run. We struggled. Larry Johnson that year had a helluva year for the Chiefs running the ball. He had a great year.

For us, winning that game and the way we won it, it really set us up to go far in the playoffs that year. Obviously we ended up winning the Super Bowl, and (the Chiefs) game really said a lot about our team, just about the way we were going to play in the playoffs. We kind of set the tone.

(The Chiefs were held to 44 rushing yards, and Johnson had just 32 on 13 carries.)

We got tired of hearing how bad we were on defense. But at the end of the day, we knew we had to get better if we were going to go where we wanted to go. Coming out in that game, man, we set a tone and we continued that tone throughout the playoffs.

You can talk about the Super Bowl and you can talk about the AFC Championship Game, but that game right there set the tone. If we didn't beat them and if we don't beat the Baltimore Ravens, we don't get there.

That game was pivotal for us.

Larry Johnson was their bell cow. That's what they were doing great that year, running the ball. This game was no different than any game for us. We had to stop the run. That was our theme. Stop the run, stop Larry Johnson, and make the quarterback beat us. Once we stopped Larry Johnson, I can remember guys just flying around, having a great time, making plays.

Everybody was doing something to help out. When you can get an offense one-dimensional—and of course you remember the type of guys we had rushing the quarterback—it makes the game a lot easier. You stop the run and make a team pass the ball, and you can turn your pass rushers loose. Rob (Mathis) and (Dwight) Freeney can just do what they always do. They raised havoc back there.

(Johnson was stopped for no gain on his first carry and managed two yards on his second.)

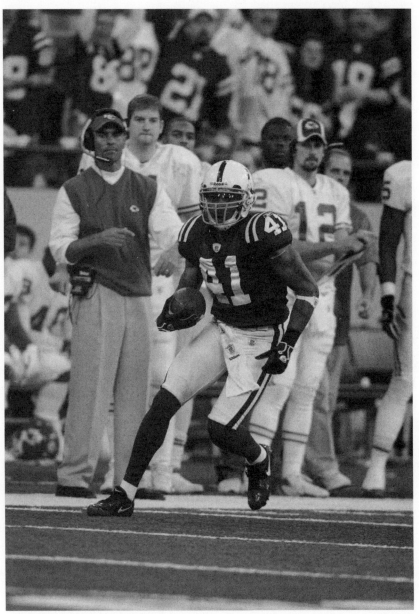

Safety Antoine Bethea attributed the Colts' world championship push in 2006 to an opening playoff win over the Kansas City Chiefs.

We set the tone right out of the gate.

(The Chiefs' offense had 16 total yards in the first half.)

We hit our stride at the right time. Everything we did worked. They weren't able to get anything going. The media and everybody were taking about how bad our run defense was, and there were times it wasn't very good at all. But holding Larry Johnson to 32 yards on 13 carries was big. Nobody thought we could do that except us.

I also think about the Kansas City game because I got my first post-season pick. I remember it like it was yesterday. It was toward the end of the game. (Quarterback Trent Green) tried to throw a "7 route" to (Samie) Parker. I was able to step in front of it and pick it off on their sideline.

I've still got the ball. I keep 'em all. It's something that you might take for granted now, but I'm pretty sure as time goes on and I get older, as I have kids and they have kids, that's something I can sit back and go down memory lane and show my kids and talk about. Just enjoy.

That game, man, the way the defense was playing, the way we were flying around, it was fun to be a part of that. That's how we knew we could play. Just the physical way we played. Just the feel of the RCA Dome that day was great.

The Aftermath

The resurgence against the Chiefs was just the beginning of a historic run for the franchise. And no one should underestimate the impact of Bethea and the defense.

During the 12–4 regular season, the run defense was categorically the NFL's worst. It allowed averages of 173 yards per game and 5.3 per attempt. It was the third-highest per-game yield in franchise history and the highest since 1978. Ten different running backs cracked the 100-yard barrier in a game, including Jones-Drew twice.

Then came the postseason.

That's when the defense transformed itself from sieve to strength. While dispatching the Chiefs, Baltimore Ravens, New England Patriots, and finally the Chicago Bears in Super Bowl XLI, the Colts hammered opponents with a relentless running game and a stout defense.

"We had a great run," Bethea said. "We got Bob back. We got Rob back. Dominic (Rhodes) and the running game really got going. They ran the ball like crazy.

"And the defense kind of hit our stride at the right time. We all took a lot of pride in that."

During the four-game playoff run, the defense limited opposing offenses to 238.5 total yards per game, including 82.8 on the ground.

"Even that second game against Baltimore, they had Jamal Lewis and he had a helluva year, as well (1,132 yards, nine touchdowns)," Bethea said.

In a 15–6 victory, the Colts held the Ravens without a touchdown and allowed Lewis 53 yards on 13 carries.

"It was great that we could really talk about holding those guys down," Bethea said. "We held Baltimore to two field goals. Even that game, the defense played the way we were supposed to play that year."

CHAPTER 13

JASON BELSER

Safety 1992–2000

December 5, 1996, vs. Philadelphia Eagles at RCA Dome

INDIANAPOLIS COLTS 37, PHILADELPHIA EAGLES 10

Ceasar Belser had been where he son was going and was quick with fatherly advice.

"My dad always told me, 'Just be the best safety on the field every game you play. You do that, you'll be fine,'" Jason Belser said.

"I told myself that was something I can manage. I knew that was something I could control."

It was the voice of experience. Ceasar Belser was selected in the 10th round of the 1966 draft by the Washington Redskins and would spend four seasons with the Kansas City Chiefs and another with the San Francisco 49ers. He passed away in March of 2016.

Jason Belser heeded his father's counsel.

"I played hard every time I was on the field," he said. "I gave it everything I had. I always made sure I had nothing left."

The Colts noticed Belser's relentless approach at Oklahoma and selected him in the eighth round of the 1992 draft with the 197th overall pick.

They never regretted the decision. Belser would appear in 141 games for them in nine seasons, 126 as a starter. He was relatively small in stature—5'9", 196 pounds—but always seemed to make a difference. His Colts résumé includes 13 interceptions, three of which he returned for touchdowns, seven forced fumbles, and 10 fumble recoveries.

Notes on Jason Belser

Joined Colts:	Selected in eighth round of 1992 draft with 197th overall pick
Jersey No.:	29
Birthdate:	May 28, 1970
Height:	5-9
Weight:	196
Games/starts with Colts:	141/126
Highlights:	One of the most productive safeties in Indianapolis Colts history. Appeared in 141 regular-season games, 126 as a starter. Started final 102 games with Colts. Piled up 979 tackles, nine sacks, and 13 interceptions. Returned three interceptions for touchdowns. Also forced seven fumbles and recovered 10 fumbles. Had at least 100 tackles in seven seasons with a team-best 118 in 1997 and 129 in '98. Recipient of team's Ed Block Courage Award in 1997 for courageous play in vote of his teammates. Was a four-year letterman and three-year starter at Oklahoma. Became only second defensive back in school history with at least 200 career tackles. Also posted 13 interceptions, 16 passes defensed, and four forced fumbles. Father, Ceasar, played in the NFL for five seasons with Kansas City Chiefs and San Francisco 49ers.

No game better exemplified Belser's presence than a 1996 meeting with the Philadelphia Eagles.

The Game
By Jason Belser

That was a very big game. One of the things I think about from my tenure with the Colts is Thursday night games, Sunday night games, Monday night games. I always tried to make the most of those opportunities. With us being a small-market club, we didn't get that many opportunities to play on national television. It wasn't just another game. I always wanted to try and put my best foot forward because I knew there was no competition for viewership.

Overall that's how our entire team approached those games. We were a smaller market, and people didn't pay a lot of attention to us. We were trying to establish ourselves as competitors in the NFL. It brought out the best in you when you knew no one else was on (TV) and the whole football community is probably watching you.

We were still sort of new to the (national TV) stage. For me, I wanted to play good in those games. That's when you got noticed. For me, the Pro Bowl never came to fruition. The closest I got was as an alternate in maybe 2000. There were always teams in the playoffs every year and their players were going. It was Blaine Bishop (Tennessee Titans) and Rod Woodson (Baltimore Ravens) and Brock Marion (Miami Dolphins). You just had to make the most of every opportunity when you were on national television.

That night against the Eagles I had a pretty good game (eight tackles, two interceptions, one returned 44 yards for a touchdown). My goal was to be the best safety on the field. Like I said, my dad simplified that for me. At that time, (the Colts) didn't have many Pro Bowlers except maybe a kicker went once or twice. Other than Marshall (Faulk), who wasn't with us much longer, we didn't have many Pro Bowlers.

So I just tried to be the best I could be. That's how I approached every game. It was a Thursday night game. Both Marshall and I were named offensive and defensive players of the game. It just worked out.

We had a fantastic game plan that night. Our defensive coordinator that year, Jim Johnson, did a great job. We wanted to play great for J. J. (The Eagles) ran a lot of crossing routes, and he allowed me to play kind of a "one-man-free" style where I was able to break on the ball on the different

In a 1996 meeting with the Philadelphia Eagles, safety Jason Belser had eight tackles and two interceptions. He returned one for a touchdown.

levels, whether it was taking away the deep cross first or the slant. He really let me figure it out. When I saw the formations, I knew where they were going to go with the ball.

Matter of fact, that's how I got the two picks. One play I remember it like it was yesterday. (Irving) Fryar is running a crossing route toward the visitor's sideline, and I just caught him right up under the chin. He was a big receiver and I almost flipped him over. That was better than the two interceptions and the one for a touchdown. It made a statement.

We just knew what we were doing. We were playing fast. We were reacting. We challenged our corners all the time, Eugene Daniel and Dedric Mathis. We were playing man-to-man and J.J. told them, "Get up on your man. You're going to have safety help, but win your individual battles." And we did. We kicked the (heck) out of them all night. We were on point.

(The Colts led, 10–3, in the second quarter when Belser intercepted a Ty Detmer pass and returned it 44 yards for a touchdown.)

I read the route and broke on the pass. I was prepared for it because we had worked on it all week. After that, the offense got rolling. We got clicking. We had an answer for everything they wanted to do. We executed about as well as you could. The Eagles were stacked. They had Fryar, Ricky Watters. Look at what they did that year (10–6 record and wild-card play-off berth). That was a darned good team and we just took it to them. We beat 'em like they stole something from us.

We were trying to establish an identity. We were young. By that time, we didn't have a lot of veteran leadership. Jeff Herrod, Eugene, and a few other (veteran) guys were there, but we were a young team trying to cement ourselves.

That was one of those games where we figured it out and things started clicking for us. That's what it was about. We just played at a high level.

The Aftermath

No one should casually dismiss the accomplishments of the Belser-led Colts that season. The lopsided win over the Eagles was part of a 9–7 record and helped propel them to their second consecutive playoff appearance.

It marked the first time since 1987–88 the Colts posted consecutive winning seasons and the first time since 1976–77 they reached the postseason in back-to-back years.

"We took pride in that," Belser said. "That was our mind-set, who we wanted to be. We knew nobody was going to give us respect. We had to go out and earn it. At that point, you still had the big guns in the league. We were dealing with Dan Marino and Jim Kelly in our division. We were the doormats. You just had to play for pride, and when you got on national television like we were against the Eagles, man, you had to make the most of it."

Belser also points to an oddity when capsulizing his nine-year stint with the Colts. During one three-year stretch, they had the wherewithal to knock off the reigning Super Bowl champions: San Francisco in 1995, Dallas in '96, and Green Bay in '97.

"Looking back at my career, I'm satisfied. I'm content. I have no regrets," Belser said. "The most important thing is I know I gave it everything I had every time I was out there."

Early in his career, Belser attempted to pattern himself after Chicago Bulls superstar Michael Jordan.

"I read every Michael Jordan book that had been written at the time," he said. "I wanted to approach football like he approached basketball. My love for the game, my knowledge of the game.

"Jordan didn't want to miss a game, ever. He didn't know if some kid was showing up from Indiana to watch him play one night. He didn't want to disappoint the kid.

"That's how I approached it. I figured I only had so many snaps in my body. For whatever number that was, I wanted to make sure I could look back on my career and could say I exhausted every bit of energy I had. I sleep very comfortably with myself."

CHAPTER 14

MARCUS POLLARD

Tight end 1995–2004
November 15, 1998, vs. New York Jets at RCA Dome
INDIANAPOLIS COLTS 24, NEW YORK JETS 23

That Marcus Pollard's collegiate résumé caught the attention of Indianapolis Colts general manager Bill Tobin was surprising more for the sport involved than the solid statistics it contained.

The 6'3", 247-pound Pollard averaged 7.3 points and 5.0 rebounds as a two-year starting power forward with Bradley University's basketball team. The Braves didn't field a football team, so he satisfied that particular itch by playing intramural flag football as a senior.

And just to remind everyone, Tobin's Colts were a football team at the highest level.

Despite not having played football since his prep days at Valley (Alabama) High School, Pollard had caught the eye of Tobin's area scout during his senior year at Bradley. The scout noticed the powerfully-built frame, the intriguing athleticism. Those characteristics, he reasoned, were ideal for an NFL tight end.

As the Colts were going through the daily grind during their 1994 training camp at Anderson (Indiana) University, Tobin decided to kick the tires on Pollard. He brought him in for a workout.

Notes on Marcus Pollard

Joined Colts:	Free agent in 1995
Jersey No.:	81
Birthdate:	February 8, 1972
Height:	6-3
Weight:	247
Games/starts with Colts:	146/102
Highlights:	Signed as a free agent in '95 after not playing football in college. Was a two-year starting power forward at Bradley University. Among tight ends in franchise history, ranks No. 3 with 263 receptions and No. 4 with 3,391 yards and 35 touchdowns. His 86-yard touchdown catch against New Orleans in 2001 is the sixth-longest reception in franchise history. Started 8 of 11 playoff games and had 16 receptions, 225 yards, and one touchdown.

"I remember everything about it," Pollard said. "It was during camp and they were having practice. They were in pads, working out. I think it was in the middle of a two-a-day (session).

"All the players were leaving the field, and I had a workout during that lunch-time break. To tell you the truth, I was expecting to get pads that day."

That wasn't the case, as Pollard soon discovered.

"Yeah, that was just my dumb mentality and way of thinking," he said. "I thought I was just going to walk out there and put some pads on. I was going to work out, show them what I could do and they were going to give me some pads.

"That wasn't the case. It was like, 'Not so fast, pal. We've got some guys out here who'll break you in half.'"

Instead, Pollard went through several drills. He ran. He lifted. He sweat under a high, hot August sky.

"I had a good 40 time. I bench-pressed 225 (pounds) nine times. I ran some routes," Pollard said. "I was just showing them my athleticism and catching the ball. I really didn't know what I was doing.

"But I showed them my athleticism. I showed them enough they offered me a contract the following year. I was a little mad going back to Peoria (Illinois). I wanted some shoulder pads and a helmet. I wanted to play right now.

"In my mind, I was ready. In their mind, I wasn't. I went back and worked out and got ready for the next year."

The Colts signed him as a free agent in January 1995, and Pollard gradually developed into one of the most productive tight ends in franchise history. His first NFL catch came at Dallas in 1996 and offered a glimpse of what was to come: a 48-yard touchdown from quarterback Jim Harbaugh.

The game that resonates loudest, though, was November 15, 1998, against the New York Jets. He had only one reception, but it was a 14-yard touchdown with 24 seconds remaining that gave the Colts a 24–23 win and quarterback Peyton Manning the first of his NFL-best 56 game-winning drives.

The Game

By Marcus Pollard

Yeah, the Jets game, no question about it. We beat the Jets and I scored the winning touchdown within the last two minutes. There was a picture in the newspaper the next day and it said, "Jet Lag." (Jets cornerback) Otis Smith almost kept me from scoring, but I had just enough of the ball across the goal line.

I don't know if it necessarily was the game that made it really special. I didn't have a single catch the whole game up to that point. One catch, one touchdown for however many yards it was. But my entire family was at the game. I remember my mom, Geraldine, my stepdad, Carl, my sister, Krisse, my grandmother, Juanita, my cousins, Pero and Carlos.

That was very unusual. They did it one game a year, and coincidentally it was that game. It was a home game for us and they took a charter bus from Alabama. It was about a fourteen-hour bus ride. I'm telling you, it was everybody. The whole clan was there. It was sixty-some people on the bus. I paid for the bus. They paid for their tickets to the game.

It ended up being an ideal situation. After I scored, I took the football and gave it to my mom. She was close enough in the stands to our bench that I actually handed her the ball I used to score the touchdown.

The pass was from Peyton and I remember it was what we called an "H-pump." I was supposed to run a 5-yard "out." The underneath corner was supposed to bite and go underneath, and I was supposed to come in behind him and hopefully score based on the coverage. Turned out I broke out five yards and he was still hounding me. I had to do a little whirlybird and got enough space so Peyton could get me the ball. Peyton kept his eyes on me. He didn't come off me. He should have come off me and gone to somebody else.

But he stayed on me and fortunately I made a little move and got open and found enough space and he got me the ball and I dragged the guy about four yards and got enough of the football over the line and broke the plane of the goal line.

It was like that the whole game. I just remember it being a struggle. The Jets were pretty good at the time (a 6–3 record) and we were kind of an up-and-coming team, trying to get good at that time (a 1–8 record).

Tight end Marcus Pollard had one reception in the Colts' 1998 win over the New York Jets, but it was a game-winning 14-yard touchdown.

Like I said, it was just a struggle for us the whole game. For me, it was not getting down. I hadn't caught a ball, hadn't done anything really special at all. And remember, my family and friends were at the game. It was all about persevering. You feel like, "Golly, I'm worthless. I haven't done anything the whole game and my whole family is in the stands . . . they came up to see me and I haven't done anything." You can almost hear them in the stands: "That's my son. That's my nephew."

To make that play at the end of the game and for us to come out victorious, it was just incredible. It was just elating because of everything that happened. The game was tough. It was a grind. I had to do something different to get open. Peyton stayed with me the entire play to get me the ball. I dragged the guy across the goal line. I give the ball to my mom. We got the victory. It was a combination of all those things. Incredible.

I was a little concerned getting together with my family after the game. But then you get the win and you score the winning touchdown. That gives you a lot to talk about. It was fantastic.

After the game we went back to my place in Carmel. Oh, we partied it up pretty good.

The Aftermath

Pollard's hardwood-to-gridiron journey was impressive. His 10-year stint with the team that gave him his NFL shot concluded in 2004, and he left footprints. Pollard ranks No. 3 with 263 receptions and No. 4 with 3,391 yards and 35 touchdowns among Colts tight ends.

"You know those commercials: Priceless," he said. "I can't put a price on my years in Indianapolis. It was priceless. To this day, I stay in touch with the friends I made while I was there—Peyton, Reggie (Wayne), Marv (Harrison), Edgerrin (James), Jeff Saturday, Tarik (Glenn), (Dwight) Freeney, and Robert Mathis, just to name a few. And to have been coached by one of the greatest, Tony Dungy.

"My affection for Indianapolis is enormous."

CHAPTER 15

MARSHALL FAULK

Running back 1994–1998

October 1, 1995, vs. St. Louis Rams at RCA Dome

INDIANAPOLIS COLTS 21, ST. LOUIS RAMS 18

He left San Diego State early, but only after leaving footprints all over the Aztecs' history books and collegiate football fields. He was a two-time NCAA rushing champion who rushed for at least 100 yards 23 times, eclipsed the 200-yard barrier on seven occasions and burst past the 300-yard mark twice. He was runner-up for the Heisman Trophy in 1992, and fourth in the '93 voting.

To the Colts, he was the Marshall Plan.

The team used the second overall pick in the 1994 draft on Marshall Faulk, and he immediately addressed so many of its needs. Primarily, he gave them a big-play threat on offense. He also provided the backfield with stability. The Colts had ranked last in the NFL in rushing in each of the previous three seasons and hadn't had a 1,000-yard rusher since Eric Dickerson in 1989.

"We needed a back to improve the running game, and in our mind, (Faulk) was the answer," coach Ted Marchibroda said at the time. "We got the football player we wanted. We got a kid who's got the speed, a kid who's a tremendous receiver and a kid who'll stick his nose in there to block."

Notes on Marshall Faulk

Joined Colts:	First-round pick in 1994, second overall selection
Jersey No.:	28
Birthdate:	February 26, 1973
Height:	5-10
Weight:	211
Games/starts with Colts:	77/76
Highlights:	Member of the Pro Football Hall of Fame's Class of 2011 following 12-year career with Colts and St. Louis Rams. Named the 2000 NFL Most Valuable Player and was a three-time Offensive Player of the Year. Ranks No. 10 in NFL history with 12,279 rushing yards, No. 4 with 19,154 yards from scrimmage, and No. 7 with 136 touchdowns. Ranks No. 3 in rushing in Colts history with 5,320 yards and No. 5 with 8,124 total yards from scrimmage. Seven-time Pro Bowl selection, including three times with Colts. Named MVP of Pro Bowl as a rookie in 1994.

Faulk was Bill Tobin's first draft pick as the Colts' general manager. He hit a home run, grand slam variety.

"I think he's going to be an outstanding player," Tobin said. "We expect him to play and play all the time."

Faulk reported to his rookie training camp in late July, and his teammates made him feel right at home. Sort of.

The other running backs huddled together on an Anderson University practice field, clasped hands, and shouted in unison, *The superback is here!*

Faulk attempted to downplay his heralded arrival.

"I don't want to set myself up on a pedestal with anyone," Faulk said. "I haven't proved myself yet. I have a ways to go."

The initial returns were encouraging.

Faulk was the NFL's consensus Rookie of the Year and earned a Pro Bowl berth. He finished fifth in the league in rushing with 1,282 yards. He eclipsed the 100-yard mark four times, including in his first two professional games.

The Marshall Plan was underway.

The Game
By Marshall Faulk

The game against the Rams in '95 was a pretty good all-around game for me. I remember we both came in with good records and I rushed for 177 yards and three touchdowns. And I know I had a pretty good first half (10 carries, 125 yards, two TDs).

It was one of those games where every decision you make is a good decision running the ball. If you make a decision, it's trying to make a better decision. You're getting 3, 4, 5 yards, or 8 and 10 yards every time. Then—*bam!*—you break off a 25-yard run. Like I said, regardless of what decision you make, it's a good one. That's the kind of feeling you have on a day like that. Everything you do is right.

It's a great feeling, man. There's really no feeling like that when you're doing it. The only thing you feel as a runner is the volume of carries. If you're up around the mid-to-late 20 (carry) mark, you start to feel that. That's what you try to condition yourself for, for when those times come around in the season when the running game is working and they want to grind things out. You want to condition your body for that.

But a day like that, I only had 19 carries. That was around average for me. There were times I went well into the 30s and felt just as good.

That's what you want. You want to make sure that you get those carries and you can handle those carries, because the yards really don't matter. It's the touches. I don't really look at yards. I look at yards per carry. How effective were you? That says a lot to me about a running back's effectiveness. In today's league, you're just not going to get a chance to get a lot of high-volume games, a high volume of carries to get your yards up.

I never carried the ball enough in my career to lead the league in rushing. Nowadays, the running back you draft or the running back that's playing for you, it's yards per carry. It shows his effectiveness. That's one of the reasons I think Trent Richardson has struggled in the league. He was a high-volume carry guy in college. He got to the league, and they just can't give you the ball enough times for you to get your yards. And he didn't have the ability to break off big runs.

(Against the Rams, Faulk averaged a staggering 9.3 yards per attempt.)

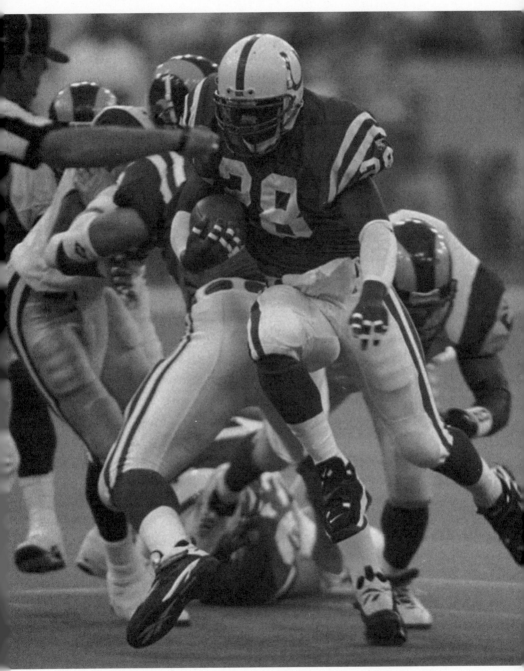

In a 1995 meeting with the St. Louis Rams, running back Marshall Faulk tormented his future employers with 177 yards and three touchdowns on 19 rushing attempts.

If you don't have early success, they'll quit giving you the ball. You won't even get 14 carries. You might not make it to 10. If you get five or six carries and you're not doing well, they'll go away from you. I'll be damned if they're going to blame the offensive line. They're going to bring in another running back and see if he has any luck.

(Included in Faulk's first five carries were 32- and 33-yard touchdowns, and another 33-yard gain.)

That's why I remember the Rams game. It was about being effective and doing as much as possible with the touches you got.

That game also was important because we were more or less still trying to establish our identity as a team. The organization had so much history, but we felt like a new franchise with the issues of leaving Baltimore and coming to Indy. It was the beginning of the tradition that started and took over in Indy with football becoming not just relevant, but the No. 1 sport in Indianapolis with the fans.

They were loyal fans in Indianapolis, but they had not experienced playoff football to the degree of success we had in '95. They got exposed to it, saw what it was like, and became enamored with it. You show some loyal fans something like what we did that season (reach the AFC title game at Pittsburgh), they get a taste of it and they want more.

From then on, we pretty much played in front of a sold-out crowd.

The Aftermath

The Marshall Plan remained viable, and often was vibrant, until the 1999 offseason. Management balked when Faulk wanted to renegotiate his contract. Faced with the prospect of their three-time Pro Bowl star staging a disruptive holdout, the Colts traded him to the Rams.

As things turned out, Faulk's career soared in St. Louis as the undeniable centerpiece for the Greatest Show on Turf. He was the NFL's 2000 MVP and a three-time Offensive Player of the Year. He helped the Rams reach the Super Bowl twice and was part of their world championship following the 1999 season. He was inducted into the Pro Football Hall of Fame as part of the Class of 2011.

But Faulk was wary when the Colts shipped him to St. Louis for second- and fifth-round draft picks.

"You want to say, 'Yeah, the Colts really looked out for Marshall. Look where they sent him,'" Faulk said with a laugh. "No. The Rams were one of the two teams that were worse than the Colts."

The Rams were 4–12 in 1998, marking the eighth time in nine seasons the franchise had lost at least 10 games. They still were trying to get settled in St. Louis after relocating from Los Angeles following the 1994 season.

"They didn't send me to a contender," Faulk said. "They weren't doing me a favor.

"But we made it work."

Faulk's arrival coincided with the unexpected emergence of quarterback Kurt Warner and addition of wide receiver Torry Holt, the sixth overall pick in the 1999 draft. Isaac Bruce already had established himself as one of the NFL's elite receivers.

The Greatest Show on Turf, noted Faulk, "wasn't the team the Colts sent me to. They didn't send me to a team that had all those components and they only needed me.

"We made it perfect."

CHAPTER 16

JERRAUD POWERS

Cornerback 2009–2012
November 15, 2009, vs. New England Patriots at Lucas Oil Stadium
INDIANAPOLIS COLTS 35, NEW ENGLAND PATRIOTS 34

The two barometers of success in the AFC were undeniable, and were getting together once again to compare résumés and swap hits.

On November 15, 2009, it was Indianapolis Colts versus New England Patriots. Again.

"Everybody's going to make this an unbelievably huge game," said Colts defensive end Raheem Brock. "It probably is, but every game's big."

But seriously, some are bigger than others. Colts versus Patriots always is bigger than most, and the collision on NBC's Sunday prime-time stage was as big as it got for a non-playoff game. The sellout crowd of 67,476 remains the largest regular-season turnout at Lucas Oil Stadium.

Listen to New England quarterback Tom Brady: "We always enjoy playing them. They're a great team. They seem to always be one of the best teams in the league. It will be a great challenge for us."

As the latest episode in the intriguing series neared, the hype machine churned.

The Colts were 8–0 and featured an all-star cast: Peyton Manning, Reggie Wayne, Dwight Freeney, Robert Mathis, Jeff Saturday.

Notes on Jerraud Powers

Joined Colts:	Third-round draft pick in 2009, 92nd overall selection
Jersey No.:	25
Birthdate:	July 19, 1987
Height:	5-10
Weight:	187
Games/starts with Colts:	42/42
Highlights:	Four-year starter who finished with 207 tackles, six interceptions, 33 defended passes, and two forced fumbles. In November 2011, intercepted a pass by Atlanta's Matt Ryan and returned it 6 yards for a touchdown. Signed with the Arizona Cardinals as an unrestricted free agent after 2012 season. In first seven seasons, appeared in 87 regular-season games, 82 as a starter. Collected 11 interceptions. Two-year starter at Auburn who started 23 of 36 career games.

The Patriots were 6–2 and following the lead of Brady, Randy Moss, Wes Welker, and Vince Wilfork.

A quick glance at the Tale of the Tape reinforced the bona fides of each franchise, and the reason the buildup could never be overstated.

Over the previous seven seasons (2002–08), the Patriots were an NFL-best 86–26. They reached the playoffs five times and advanced to the Super Bowl on three occasions, winning a pair of world championships. The Colts were a tick behind at 85–27 in the regular season. They reached the playoffs each year and won their first world title in more than three decades when they handled the Chicago Bears 29–17 in Super Bowl XLI after the '06 season.

But a closer look reveals the foundation for the mutual respect among organizations and combative relationship between fan bases.

When New England won consecutive Super Bowl titles after the '03 and '04 seasons, it used the Colts as postseason stepping-stones. That included a 24–14 decision in the '03 AFC title game in Foxboro, Massachussets.

And when they Colts captured their world title three years later, the biggest and most satisfying step was taken in the '06 conference championship game. It came at the expense of the Patriots in Indianapolis.

"At the time, they were our nemesis," said cornerback Jerraud Powers, a rookie in 2009. "We knew they were the team we had to deal with to get to where we wanted to go."

November 15, 2009 came down to 4th-and-2.

The Game

By Jerraud Powers

Yeah, it was the game Bill Belichick went for it on 4th-and-2. Nobody could believe it.

(The Patriots led, 34–28, with 2:08 remaining but faced a 4th-and-2 at their own 28-yard line.)

Percentages say punt the ball, of course. But I guess when you've got Peyton over there, it doesn't matter if you punt it or go for it. He's capable of doing what Peyton does if you give him the chance.

I think it was just one of those gut feelings Belichick went with. I don't think it was a bad call by him by any means. If he had punted it, I don't think it would have been any different. Like I said, Peyton is capable of doing special things if you give him enough time. Their offense had been clicking all day. When (the Patriots) have arguably the best quarterback in the league, as well, in Tom Brady, you do what he did. "I believe in my offense. I believe in my guy. I think we can get two yards."

We knew what was at stake when we went out for that last series. It was one of those situations where it was do-or-die. It wasn't like nobody was nervous or anything like that. We just knew our backs were to the wall and we had to make a play. There wasn't any talking or any extra "We need to do this. We need to do that." We just made our calls and went out there and played. We knew the situation. We knew the yards they needed to get. We knew there was going to be some type of quick passing just to get the first down.

Man, I almost came up with the big play (on 3rd-and-2). Wes (Welker) tried to run a quick little option route on me and I jumped it. It went right through my hands. I should have caught it. I was kind of ticked that I didn't make the play. It would have been one of those balls that I would have hung in my office for sure, me getting a pick-6 off Tom. I was ticked because you just don't know what's going to happen on the next play. I felt like an opportunity just slipped by. I wasn't so mad at myself. I was just mad I wasn't able to make a play for the team in a situation we needed it. I was definitely relieved after Melvin (Bullitt) made his play.

On 4th-and-2, it was right there. It was our job to make that one last stop. We were fortunate enough to make the stop. If they get it, they make the first down, the game's over, and everybody's going to say it was a great call by Bill Belichick.

You know Bill. He had confidence in his offense they could get two yards. A lot of people looked at it like he was disrespecting our defense, but I thought it was one of those situations where he believed his offense was good enough to get those two yards. And they almost did.

We were just trying to play the percentages, play off what we saw on film. Guys just stepped up and made a play. I was split out wide (left) on Wes Welker. He ran a quick out, I believe. They tried to get Kevin Faulk matched up on Melvin on another quick little option route, and Melvin was able to tackle him. I remember Faulk juggling the ball and he was short (of the first down).

I was worried. If you look at the replay, I'm right behind the official who's measuring. I'm holding my hand in the air because I thought he had it for a second. I wasn't sure about the rule or how it worked with juggling the catch. Once he was declared short, I just took off running toward the fans. It was a great feeling. You would have thought we just won the Super Bowl.

Then, Peyton did his thing (game-winning 1-yard touchdown pass to Reggie Wayne with 13 seconds to play).

I do remember they got out on us pretty quick. Everything happened so fast. Randy caught a couple of big plays in our cover-2 system and Tom was just on fire. He was hitting on all cylinders. But once we got into the locker room at half (trailing 24–14), Coach (Jim) Caldwell settled us down. Everybody remembers how calm he used to be. He was cut from that Tony Dungy era. He kept saying, "We're going to win the game. We're going to win the game. Just relax and do what you do."

The offense started clicking, and the defense started getting stops and getting Peyton the ball a little more. Before you know it, it's a dogfight. I was happy the defense came up at the end and made some plays. We'd get overshadowed so much because of Peyton and the offense. It was great to know the defense made the plays that won the game.

Cornerback Jerraud Powers (25) and safety Melvin Bullitt played key roles as the Colts beat the Patriots in the legendary "4th-and-2" meeting in 2009.

The Aftermath

The ripple effects of 4th-and-2 impacted a team and a player.

The Colts became the first team in league history to open 9–0 for the third time in five seasons. Their unbeaten streak would reach 14 before management chose caution over attempting to join the 1972 Miami Dolphins as the only teams in NFL history to navigate a season undefeated.

After tapping the brakes and losing the final two games of the regular season, the Colts regrouped and reached Super Bowl XLIV by rolling past Baltimore, 20–3, in the AFC divisional round and the New York Jets, 30–17, in the conference championship game.

Powers, meanwhile, established himself as someone to be reckoned with.

The third-round draft pick out of Auburn arrived in Indianapolis mature beyond his years. He secured a starting spot during his first NFL training camp and developed into a defensive cornerstone. Powers finished sixth on the team with 71 tackles and added one interception.

Advice from team president Bill Polian during training camp helped accelerate Powers's emergence.

"I had a good day at camp, and the next day Bill Polian told me to follow Reggie Wayne wherever he went," he said of the team's perennial Pro Bowl receiver. "So I did. I followed Reggie, and I think I picked off Peyton maybe once or twice that day.

"From that day forward, I was the starter in the first preseason game. I still had to prove myself, but I knew I belonged. Once you get the approval from Bill, you know you've kind of arrived a little bit. Nobody knows football like Bill knows football."

Before leaving Indianapolis as a free agent following the '12 season—he signed with the Arizona Cardinals—Powers would start 42 regular-season games and contribute six interceptions to a team that reached the playoffs three times.

The ability to rise to the Patriots' challenge in '09 was critical to his development.

"I was a starter and played well that year," Powers said. "But going up against Randy Moss, Tom Brady, and all those guys for the first time, that was really special. It was kind of like an eye-opener for me. To be able to make a few plays that game and make a couple of plays on Randy . . . and (the announcers) were talking great about me on TV.

"It was an eye-opener for me, it really was. It was like a welcome-to-the-NFL type of moment for me.

"To beat them how we beat them and go on and win 14 straight games that year and get to the Super Bowl, that was really a special time."

A hamstring injury kept Powers out of the final two games of the regular season, and he suffered a fractured left foot in the playoff game against the Ravens that required surgery prior to the Super Bowl.

Yet Powers returned.

"Trust me, I wasn't going to miss that," he said of the 31–17 loss to the New Orleans Saints in Super Bowl XLIV. "It was a great year, probably one of the greatest years I'll remember when I'm done playing."

CHAPTER 17

BRANDON STOKLEY

Wide receiver 2003–2006
January 4, 2004, vs. Denver Broncos at RCA Dome
2003 AFC Wild Card Playoffs
INDIANAPOLIS COLTS 41, DENVER BRONCOS 10

The expectations and accompanying pressure were reaching levels that made breathing difficult.

Brandon Stokley had nothing to do with the Indianapolis Colts' prior playoff futility—three one-and-done exits since quarterback Peyton Manning's heralded arrival in 1998—but understood what was at stake as their January 4, 2004, wild-card matchup with the Denver Broncos neared. A year prior to the day, the Colts were handed their worst playoff loss ever—41–0 to the New York Jets.

"Yeah, I remember a lot of buildup to the (Broncos) game," said Stokley, who signed as a free-agent wide receiver during the '03 offseason. "Peyton had never won a playoff game, and the year before they lost to the Jets in the first round.

"There was a bunch of talk about, 'Can Peyton get over the hump and win a playoff game?' It was hard not to hear that."

Stokley and Manning were friends before becoming teammates, yet their casual conversations seldom dealt with Manning's playoff troubles.

"He always handles his stuff pretty well," Stokley said. "It wasn't anything that was talked about. We're good friends, so I know what's being said about him in the media.

"As a friend outside of football, I wanted to be a part of helping alleviate those questions for him. A lot of other guys were the same way."

Cranking up the fan base's anxiety level a notch or two was the fact that Denver posted a 31–17 win over the Colts, in the RCA Dome no less, two weeks earlier.

"They handed it to us pretty good," Stokley said. "I just remember we had a chip on our shoulder about that. That added more to it."

The Colts didn't stand pat. Intent on fixing what was obviously broken in the regular-season loss to Denver, the coaching staff moved center Jeff Saturday to right guard to deal with Trevor Pryce, the Broncos' disruptive defensive lineman.

Saturday helped neutralize Pryce, and the Colts en masse overwhelmed Denver. The 41–10 victory was their first playoff win since the 1995 postseason and their first at home since 1970.

Stokley played a key role—four receptions, 144 yards, including 31- and 87-yard touchdowns—as Manning won his first postseason game. The yardage is the sixth-highest total in the franchise's playoff history, while the 87-yard TD is the longest.

Notes on Brandon Stokley

Joined Colts:	Signed as a free agent March 14, 2003
Jersey No.:	83
Birthdate:	June 23, 1976
Height:	5-11
Weight:	197
Games/starts with Colts:	41/11
Highlights:	Excelled as a slot receiver alongside outside threats Marvin Harrison and Reggie Wayne. In 41 regular-season games, had 139 receptions for 1,916 yards and 15 touchdowns. Had most productive season in 16-year NFL career in 2004, when he had 68 catches for 1,077 yards and 10 touchdowns. Joined Harrison and Wayne to become the first trio in league history with at least 1,000 yards and 10 touchdowns in the same season. Appeared in six playoff games and posted 22 receptions for 333 yards and three touchdowns. His 144-yard game against Denver in 2003 playoffs ranks No.6 in franchise history, while his 87-yard touchdown against the Broncos is the longest in the team's playoff history. Originally drafted by the Baltimore Ravens in the fourth round of the 1999 draft (No. 105 overall). Appeared in 152 games during NFL career with Colts, Ravens, Denver, the New York Giants, and Seattle. Three-year standout at Louisiana-Lafayette. Set every school receiving record with 241 receptions, 3,702 yards, and 25 touchdowns.

The Game

By Brandon Stokley

What a game. I had two touchdowns in the first half, a 31-yarder for a 7–0 lead and an 87-yarder near the end of the first half. That was the longest touchdown of my career. That's a tough one to beat, you know?

Coming out of the gates, we were just on fire. Everything worked. It was awesome to be a part of that, winning Peyton's first playoff game and being a part of it and having those two touchdowns in the first half.

We were on a mission. We came out focused, and we were just clicking on all cylinders. Everybody was on top of his game. You hear about guys being in a zone. That's how that game was for all of us. You know, everything you do works. Offensively, it was like nobody could stop us. Lots of fun when it goes like that.

I remember my dad (Nelson) being there. I remember getting with him after the game and walking out of the stadium together. All the fans were there, and they were all fired up. It was just a great moment and a great feeling.

When we played Denver at the end of the season, I struggled a little bit (one catch, five yards). Just wasn't quite myself. I wanted to come out and have a great game and play well. On the 31-yard touchdown, they had a good nickel back who was on me. I beat him off the line of scrimmage and I was running a crossing route. I caught about a 14-to-18-yard pass and just turned it up the sideline on their side of the field.

It was good to get out early, especially when it was against a team that had beaten us like they had a few weeks earlier. To get out early and sort of set the tempo for the game was always big.

We just kept it rolling from there. The first half was "just" . . . "just" one of those times when you're just in a zone.

The 87-yarder was right before halftime. I remember us getting the ball back with about two minutes left and thinking, "OK, what are we going to do? Are we going to try to run the clock out and go into halftime?" Of course, Peyton never thought that way.

We were going out of the tunnel (end of the field) and I was on the left side. I had a post pattern. There's not much to it.

I remember the play was called, and I was kind of surprised when I saw the defense they were playing. They were in cover-2 defense. I think Al Wilson was supposed to be down the middle of the field as the middle linebacker. The two safeties were wide. Sometimes that middle linebacker is just fast and he gets deep so I've got no chance to get the ball. It's just a check-down to the running back in the soft cover-2.

In that down-and-distance (1st-and-10 at the Colts' 13-yard line), a lot of teams play cover-2 and just try to keep everything in front of them. I recognized it right away. Sometimes at the snap of the ball, that middle linebacker just flies out of there (trying to cover deep). They don't want to let a receiver get behind them. When I notice (Wilson) hesitate and saw the two safeties split, I'm like, "Oh, this has got a good chance."

It usually doesn't come together like that. But Peyton had enough time, made a great throw, and I didn't fall down. That was a cool play. I've never had any kind of touchdown that long.

You pretty much knew right then and there the game's over. You didn't think they had a chance to make a run at us.

For all those reasons, that's why that game was so special. Like I said, my father, who has passed away, was there, and it was special to spend time with him.

Also, I went through a lot that year. I was hurt. I was coming off Lisfranc (foot) surgery. I hurt my hamstring. It took me seven or eight games to get going and get into the lineup, so to go into the playoffs and be able to make that type of impact was pretty special. That first game for me was really special just for everything we've talked about. It was Peyton's first playoff win, and we all took pride in being part of that. He's won a lot since then, but at the time it was big news. That's what a lot of people were talking about.

It's funny, but I don't remember there being a sense of relief in the locker room after the game. Everybody was just excited. We were just all fired up. Just pretty much a young football team that got its first playoff win. It doesn't get much better than that.

You just try to keep things going. When you're in that moment, you're really excited. It was an exciting time to be a Colts football player. I remember leaving that stadium with my dad, and the fans were incredible. I remember thinking, "Man, it doesn't get much better than this." It was special.

But come Monday, you move on. It's on to the next one.

One of the offensive stars in the Colts' 41–10 rout of Denver in the 2003 playoffs was wide receiver Brandon Stokley, who contributed four catches, 144 yards, and two touchdowns.

The Aftermath

Stokley's monster game and Manning's first playoff victory were the first steps in a what-might-have-been postseason journey.

After dismantling the Broncos, the Colts went to Kansas City and held off the No. 2-seeded Chiefs, 38–31. The offense continued to purr. In two playoff games, Manning completed 44 of 56 passes (78.6 percent) for 681 yards with eight touchdowns, no interceptions, and a ridiculous 156.9 passer rating. Stokley caught eight passes for 201 yards and three touchdowns.

"It was pretty fun," Stokley said. "We didn't punt for two straight games. Think about that. That's hard to do anytime, let alone the playoffs."

The end came in with a 24–14 loss at New England in the AFC Championship Game. The offense never got untracked against the Patriots' pressure defense. To this day, the Colts and their fan base remain convinced the officials allowed the Patriots to get too physical in covering Stokley, Marvin Harrison, Reggie Wayne, Marcus Pollard, and Manning's other receivers.

"I'm still a little bitter about that one," Stokley said. "The refs swallowed their whistles and decided not to throw flags. I just remember Marcus Pollard running down the middle of the field and just getting mugged and no flags were coming.

"It was a weird game. You think back, 'How in the world do you not call some of those pass interferences?'"

Despite the frustrating finish in Foxboro, Massachusetts, Stokley and the Colts were able to use it as a springboard to future success. In '04, Manning broke Dan Marino's long-standing single-season touchdown record with 49. Stokley, Harrison, and Wayne became the first teammates in NFL history with at least 1,000 yards and 10 touchdowns each in the same season.

"I felt healthy. I felt good," Stokley said. "We showed what we could do in those playoff games, and it carried over to '04."

CHAPTER 18

ZACK CROCKETT

Running back 1995–1998

December 31, 1995, vs. San Diego Chargers at Jack Murphy Stadium

1995 AFC Wild Card Playoffs

INDIANAPOLIS COLTS 35, SAN DIEGO CHARGERS 20

The San Diego Chargers never saw it coming, but that was on them.

Two weeks before being run over by Zack Crockett in a wild-card play-off game, the Chargers experienced the full extent of the rookie fullback's 1995 regular-season rushing output.

"I think I had something like two carries," Crockett said, flashing back to the Indianapolis Colts' December 17 meeting with the Chargers in the RCA Dome.

No, it wasn't that many.

"Ok, one," he said with a laugh. "I gave myself more than I had."

One carry. Zero yards. For the record, Crockett's first NFL rushing attempt came in the fourth quarter against San Diego, on second-and-goal from the Chargers 1-yard line. He was smothered for no gain.

Crockett was a third-round draft pick who found himself languishing on the depth chart behind Pro Bowl halfback Marshall Faulk and fullback Roosevelt Potts, a 1993 second-round pick. Yet he never went through the motions as the season unfolded. The former Florida State standout realized his time would come.

"The thing is, everyone knew the type of talent I had," Crockett said. "Coach (Gene) Huey saw at the Senior Bowl what to expect. He coached me at the Senior Bowl.

"For the Colts to draft me and give me the opportunity and give my family the opportunity was the best thing that could happen to me. I had family in Indiana. It was just perfect for me."

Notes on Zack Crockett

Joined Colts:	Third-round draft pick in 1995, 79th overall selection.
Jersey No.:	32
Birthdate:	December 2, 1972
Height:	6-2
Weight:	240
Games/starts with Colts:	39/17
Highlights:	Set Colts' postseason records with 147 rushing yards and a 66-yard touchdown in 1995 wild-card game at San Diego. Also had a 33-yard touchdown against the Chargers. Rushed for 469 yards and one touchdown and caught 29 passes for 244 yards and one touchdown in 39 regular-season appearances with the Colts. NFL career encompassed 13 seasons and stints with Colts, Jacksonville Jaguars, Oakland Raiders, and Tampa Bay Buccaneers. Career totals include 1,701 rushing yards, 47 touchdowns, and 96 receptions for 680 yards and two TDs. Was a two-year letterman and one-year starter at Florida State. His brother, Henri, was a fourth-round draft pick of the Atlanta Falcons in 1997.

The NFL is all about a player seizing the moment, making the most of whatever opportunity comes his way.

For Crockett, that meant maximizing every repetition in practice while Faulk, Potts, and Lamont Warren did the heavy lifting during games. Faulk would eclipse the 1,000-yard for a second consecutive season (1,078) and earn a second straight Pro Bowl nod. Potts and Warren would be the complementary backs, combining to rush 112 times for 461 yards.

But as the season wore on, Faulk was dealing with a nagging knee injury that limited his availability. Potts suffered a season-ending knee injury in late December.

When the Colts made a late-season push and earned a wild-card playoff berth, they still were leaning on Faulk with frequent doses of Warren.

Crockett waited patiently, offering what was asked of him as a lead blocker and on special teams.

Finally, he would get his chance in the wild-card playoff game at San Diego's Jack Murphy Stadium.

Crockett seized the moment. He rushed 13 times for 147 yards, including touchdown runs of 33 and 66 yards. The yardage remains a franchise postseason record, as does the 66-yard TD.

The Game
By Zack Crockett

You just never know which rookie or which kid you've never heard about or which "walk-on" is going to step up when it matters. That's what's great about this game. When it's your turn, be ready. Always be ready. Even when you're behind someone like Marshall Faulk, you're only one play away.

I talk with (former Colts director of football operations) Bill Tobin all the time about the San Diego playoff game. Before the game, we're sitting outside on the field stretching, and he came up and touched me on the shoulder. Bill was like, "Be ready. We're going to need you today."

I knew if you're not ready to perform, they'll move on to someone else. From that moment Bill touched me on my shoulder and told me, "Hey, we need you," it was like, "OK, it's time to step on the stage." That was the game that really set my career off and pushed the fast-forward button. That was the game that springboarded my career.

(On the first play of the game, Faulk rushed for 16 yards but aggravated the injury to his left knee. He did not return.)

They knew he probably wasn't going to last. My goodness, Marshall was an outstanding talent. But the good thing about it was I was a dual-position player. I played fullback and tailback. I blocked for him and did other things. One thing about the backfield group was we had one another's back. Marshall, Lamont Warren, Cliff Groce, Rosey Potts. We all supported one another. We all wanted to see the other guys succeed.

It was pretty amazing to get that opportunity to go out there and strut your stuff and not really have any expectations. That was unbelievable. You've just got to go out there and play the game of football that you love. Things just opened up. To come out and play that game like that and for things to happen like they did to that level, it was just amazing.

This was a game I had been playing since I was a kid. You went out and had fun. Once you get out there on the field, it's like sandlot football. You go out there, they hand the ball off to you like they've done all your life, and you get it and go.

You go out and show what you're made of. You show your determination, your will, that you know what to do to execute the play. For the team to believe in me to get it done meant so much to me.

(On his 13 carries and 147 yards:)

Not bad. And I had some long ones, too, to show off my speed. I ran away from 'em.

I remember my touchdowns like it was yesterday. On the first one (33 yards), I went to the left and then I saw (linebacker) Junior Seau right there. I gave him an "out" look—a head fake like I was taking it outside—and then broke it back to the right across the middle. It was a footrace from then on. I knew they weren't going to catch me with my speed.

(On the record 66-yard TD early in the fourth quarter with the Colts ahead, 21–20:)

That one, I just hit it. I mean, I hit it. When people looked at my size, they didn't think I could run that fast. That time it was like, "Whoa! We knew he could run, but uh-oh!"

On any given day, you never knew who was going to step up and do something to help us win. That year, Jim Harbaugh was just incredible. He was Captain Comeback. You never knew if he was going to be ready to play the next week, but the guy was relentless as a quarterback. The belief in him was tremendous.

Fortunately for me, that day (in San Diego), it was my time.

Marshall and I always have been close friends. He was in my ear all day. He was in my corner. He kept telling me, "Keep it up. We need more out of you." That meant a lot.

When the game was over, I think most of America was dropping their mugs and glasses on the floor, shattering everything. We shocked everyone. Everybody had penciled in San Diego to go on to the next round. No one expected us to do anything. I can't tell you how great it felt to go out and do what we did.

We were an underdog team in an underdog year. Everybody was an unsung hero that year. And everyone in some form or fashion contributed that year. We were a *team*.

After carrying the ball once as a rookie during the regular season, fullback Zack Crockett erupted for a franchise playoff record 147 yards and two touchdowns against San Diego in the first round of the 1995 playoffs.

The Aftermath

That few outside the organization gave the Colts much of a chance to make a deep playoff run in 1995 was understandable. They needed a 10–7 win over the New England Patriots on the final day of the regular season to finish 9–7 and earn a wild-card berth.

They were double-digit underdogs at San Diego and faced similar steep odds the following week with another road test, this time against Kansas City. The Chiefs were the AFC's No. 1 seed and posted a league-best 13–3 record.

Another upset—this time by a 10–7 score at Kansas City's arctic Arrowhead Stadium— delivered the Colts to Pittsburgh for the AFC Championship Game, where their magic run ended with a 20–16 loss.

Crockett's smile widened as he relived one of the more improbable but inspiring playoff runs in NFL history.

"We were riding high," he said. "We were the team everybody didn't give a chance. We take care of business in San Diego, then we go to Kansas City, and it was probably about 15 below zero.

"We upset them in that stadium. Man, it was unbelievable. We definitely shocked the world. Then we go against Pittsburgh and I'm still thinking Aaron Bailey caught that ball."

The Colts waived Crockett early in the 1998 season, and he was claimed by the Jacksonville Jaguars. His career stabilized, though, when he signed with the Oakland Raiders in 1999. He would remain in Oakland for eight seasons and appear in 125 games, 40 as a starter, and rush for 1,232 yards with 35 touchdowns.

Crockett remains a scout with the Raiders.

And to think that '95 playoff game at San Diego probably was the trigger for what was to come.

"I just love being around the game," Crockett said. "I love to continue to learn and grow and see young guys come into this game like I did and prove themselves.

"I love to see guys who are young and raw and just want the opportunity to show what they can do. I can relate."

CHAPTER 19

BILL BROOKS

Wide receiver 1986–1992

September 30, 1990, vs. Philadelphia Eagles at Veterans Stadium

INDIANAPOLIS COLTS 24, PHILADELPHIA EAGLES 23

There was no ignoring reality as the Colts prepared for the 1990 season, their seventh in Indianapolis.

"Going into the season, we felt pretty good about ourselves with the talent we had and hopefully building off of the three previous seasons," recalled Bill Brooks, the team's veteran receiver at the time. "We were 8–8 the year before, and there were a couple of games we let get away from us."

The improvement in the NFL's newest franchise was gradual, but clear. From a 3–13 finish in 1986 that cost coach Rod Dowhower his job, the Colts followed the lead of Ron Meyer, a master motivator, to a 9–6 record and playoff berth in the strike-shortened '87 season. Then came a 9–7 record in '88 and an 8–8 mark in '89.

Further hyping optimism was the addition of Jeff George, the hometown quarterback out of Warren Central High School, as the first overall pick in the 1990 draft. He and running back Eric Dickerson were supposed to represent the foundation of future success.

"That really increased expectations," Brooks said. "We had traded (Pro Bowl offensive tackle) Chris Hinton and we got Jeff. Expectations were high. Jeff was a talented, talented quarterback. We were looking for big things from all of us, the whole team.

Notes on Bill Brooks

Joined Colts:	Fourth-round pick in 1986, 86th overall selection.
Jersey No.:	80
Birthdate:	April 6, 1964
Height:	6-0
Weight:	188
Games/starts with Colts:	106/98
Highlights:	Was the first player added to the team's Ring of Honor, joining late owner Robert Irsay in 1998. Led the team in receptions four times and in receiving yards on five occasions. Had a career-best 1,131 receiving yards as a rookie in 1986. At the time, yardage total was third-most by a rookie in NFL history. Broke franchise rookie records with 65 receptions and 1,131 yards. Ranks No. 5 in team history with 411 receptions and No. 6 with 5,818 yards. His 84-yard touchdown at San Francisco in '86 is tied for the ninth-longest in team history. Standout at Boston University. Finished career with 228 receptions, 3,579 yards, and 32 touchdowns. Excelled as a senior with 79 receptions, 1,210 yards, and 11 TDs.

"So we felt pretty good going into the season, especially starting off with two early games against the AFC East."

Optimism quickly gave way to increased anxiety, and mounting pressure on Meyer. The Colts lost their opener at Buffalo, 26–10, and followed with setbacks at home to the Patriots (16–14) and at Houston (24–10).

Players realized the season was on the verge of slipping away, and that might have included impatient owner Robert Irsay firing Meyer.

"We knew what was at stake when we did not get off to a good start," Brooks said.

Next up: Buddy Ryan's Philadelphia Eagles at Veterans Stadium. The Eagles had reached the playoffs the two previous seasons and had posted an 11–5 record in '89. The Colts were hardly comforted by the fact that Philadelphia had stumbled out of the gate, losing two of three.

"They had Buddy Ryan, and he was always known for his defenses," Brooks said. "We just weren't playing well at the time. We knew we had to pick up our game.

"We knew we had our work cut out for us."

In a game that temporarily quieted their critics, the Colts found a way.

More to the point, Brooks and quarterback Jack Trudeau found a way to generate a frenetic closing kick. Brooks caught six passes for 68 yards on the game-winning drive and capped it with a 6-yard touchdown as time expired.

The Game
By Bill Brooks

Philadelphia was loaded. They had that great defense with Reggie White, Clyde Simmons, and the rest.

I don't know if we played one of our better games that day. We just found a way. We didn't play that well. We couldn't run the ball (52 yards on 14 carries). They obviously had a pretty good defense against the run. Albert (Bentley) had a hard time getting anything going. And if I'm not mistaken, we had something like five fumbles. We only lost one, but it's hard to get anything going when you fumble five times in a game. We just didn't take care of the ball that well.

We ended up winning but we struggled all day. Give them credit, they played well and had a lot to do with how we played. It was one of those games where you just find a way.

(The Colts trailed, 23-17, with 1:51 to play. They took possession at their own 18-yard line.)

We had 82 yards to go and we were down six points, so we knew we had to score a touchdown. A field goal wasn't going to do it for us. We just marched down the field. Jack led us down the field. We had confidence. We knew we had scored on a couple of plays. Albert finally got loose for a long run (a 26-yard touchdown), and Jessie Hester had scored (a 5-yard touchdown catch from Trudeau). We knew we could do it. We just weren't quite sure how we were going to do it.

It was just a matter of sustaining the drive. We had to keep on getting first downs, keep on moving the chains. When there's only a minute and some-odd seconds left, you really have to manage the clock. That was our biggest concern, the time on the clock.

(Brooks had two catches for 24 yards in the first half, but none in the second half until the final drive. Trudeau completed 7 of 13 passes on the drive and was 6 of 7 when targeting Brooks.)

I don't remember Jack ever saying anything to me in the huddle or to me on the sideline. The only thing he probably said to all of us was, "Everyone be ready. Everyone be alert." He didn't say that to me, but to all the offensive players.

For whatever reason, he kept throwing me the ball and I tried to make sure I got open and caught the ball and got first downs. I was more concerned about getting first downs and us keeping the ball and keeping the chains moving so we could at least get in a position to score a touchdown.

Even though I hadn't had any catches in the second half until that drive, you have to keep your head in the game. I was always brought up to believe that you never know which play is going to be the one that makes the big difference. You have to play each play like it's the most important play. I kept my head in the game. I tried to understand what the defense was doing to us, how they were defending us in certain situations. I just kept doing what I was supposed to do —blocking when we were running the ball and also running my routes to make sure I was getting other people open if possible.

That's part of being a team. Some days you're going to get a lot of balls thrown to you, other days you might not get any balls thrown to you. You have to just keep plugging away.

We were able to get a first down on a 4th-and-2 (a 6-yard reception with 33 seconds to play), and that was obviously huge. If we don't get that one, the game's over. We just made a play. If someone doesn't do his job— if I don't run my route properly or if the offensive line doesn't give Jack enough time—we go home and we're 0–4.

(On the 2nd-and-goal play at the 6 with five seconds to play:)

I knew that was either going to be the last play or we might have one more chance if the play doesn't take too long. But I was thinking it was going to be our last play of the game.

As a kid, you dreamed about that, scoring the winning touchdown on the last play of the game. At the time, I wasn't thinking about that. I was more concerned about just sticking to my basic fundamentals. I was thinking about the play that's being called, my alignment, my assignment, will I have to make an adjustment based on the defense, then executing my route. Once the ball is thrown, make sure I get open and give the quarterback a good target and catch the ball.

I might have run a curl route. We were at the 6-yard line and actually the route tells me to go 12 yards. But I knew if I went 12 yards, I'm going 6 yards into the end zone. A good defender is going to play me between me and the quarterback and make it very difficult for me to come back for the ball.

I just pretty much ran and bumped into him and kind of bumped him back a little bit. I turned and Jack put the ball down by my knees, which was the right place to throw it. If I don't catch it, no one's going to catch it. I just held onto it and we scored.

Wide receiver Bill Brooks scored the game-winning touchdown in a 1990 win at Philadelphia.

Once I saw the referee throw his hands up and signal a touchdown—and I'm not proud of this—I lost track of the score, I guess. I thought the game was over and we had won. I forgot we had to kick the extra point to win the game. I ran to the opposite end zone where our tunnel was and got off the field. I waited in the locker room for a while. I was in there thinking, "Wow, guys are taking a long time to get in here." Then it dawned on me what I did. We still had to kick the extra point to win the game. I didn't go back out. By the time I was getting ready to go out, the guys started coming in.

That was strange. It was just a special game. I don't remember any other game in the pros, not like that, where I scored the winning touchdown with no time on the clock.

The Aftermath

Brooks wasn't a one-hit wonder. In fact, his name always will hold a prominent place in franchise history.

In 1998, he and late owner Robert Irsay were the first two members of the Colts' Ring of Honor. Heading into the 2016 season, Brooks is one of eleven men whose name is affixed to the lower façade at Lucas Oil Stadium.

"It was a huge honor," he said. "There were a lot of great players who came through here: Albert Bentley, Jim Harbaugh, Ray Donaldson, Eugene Daniel, Duane Bickett. They all were real good players.

"I was just honored that Jim Irsay decided to place me up there in the Ring of Honor. Believe me, it's something that I definitely am thankful for and appreciate.

"It's hard to explain what it means to me. I cherish it."

Brooks ranks No. 5 in franchise history with 411 receptions and No. 6 with 5,818 yards. His 65 receptions and 1,131 yards in 1986 remain Colts' rookie records. His eight touchdowns that season are tied with Hall of Famer Marvin Harrison's for most by a Colts rookie.

"Stats are great and all that," Brooks said, "but I'm more thankful for the players I played with and the relationships you have from that. That's what you remember.

"God truly blessed me to play as long as I did, to play here as long as I did and just have an opportunity to play. I'm thankful."

CHAPTER 20

MARK HERRMANN

Quarterback 1983–1984, 1990–1992

September 6, 1992, vs. Cleveland Browns at Hoosier Dome

INDIANAPOLIS COLTS 14, CLEVELAND BROWNS 3

Maybe it was penance for having left Baltimore after the 1983 season and settling in Indianapolis. Whatever the reason, the Colts had fallen into a frustrating rut in their new hometown.

For eight consecutive seasons following their move from Baltimore, preseason optimism quickly gave way to regular-season reality. The Colts lost eight consecutive openers.

"Oh, we all knew that," quarterback Mark Herrmann said. "You want to win that opening game and you want to win it at home. It's always a good step for the season and a momentum-builder and all that.

"You don't want to start the season with a bad taste in your mouth."

Yet they did. For eight straight seasons and with six different starting quarterbacks: Mike Pagel, Art Schlichter, Gary Hogeboom (twice), Jack Trudeau, Chris Chandler, and Jeff George (twice).

Why would anyone expect a different outcome in 1992? The Colts were coming off a league-worst 1–15 finish in 1991 and faced the Bernie Kosar-led Cleveland Browns in the '92 opener.

To complicate matters, the Colts would be without starter George, out with a thumb injury, and backup Trudeau, mired in a contract dispute.

Next up? Mark Herrmann.

Notes on Mark Herrmann

Joined Colts: Initially acquired by the Baltimore Colts in 1983 trade with Denver that sent John Elway to the Broncos; claimed off waivers from Los Angeles Rams September 4, 1990.

Jersey No.:	9
Birthdate:	January 8, 1959
Height:	6-4
Weight:	200
Games/starts with Colts:	11/4
Highlights:	Appeared in 40 games, 12 as a starter, during 11-year NFL career. Along with two stints with the Colts, spent time with the Denver Broncos, Los Angeles Rams, and San Diego Chargers. Started four of 11 games with the Baltimore/Indianapolis Colts and was 2–2 as a starter. Passed for 4,015 yards and 16 touchdowns with 36 interceptions during NFL career. Was a four-year starter at Purdue and finished collegiate career with nine NCAA, six Big Ten, and 23 Purdue passing records. Passed for 9,946 yards and 67 touchdowns during career. Finished fourth in the Heisman Trophy voting as a senior. Selected Offensive MVP in 1978 Peach Bowl, '79 Bluebonnet Bowl, and '80 Liberty Bowl.

The local icon—Purdue University and Carmel High School—hadn't started a game since 1987, when he was with the San Diego Chargers. He hadn't led a team to victory since '85, again with the Chargers.

Herrmann was efficient in what would be his final NFL start, and appearance (more on that later). He passed for 177 yards with one touchdown and one interception, and the Colts ended their season-opening dry spell with a 14–3 victory over the Browns.

The Game

By Mark Herrmann

First of all, I was surprised I was starting the game. Ted Marchibroda started me in the last preseason game against Kansas City that year. Then he said, "We want you to start the opening game." So, yeah, that was a little bit of a shock. I just started preparing myself mentally and did everything I could that week to get myself ready.

I felt like they went with me not out of desperation or anything, but because they believed I could do the job. I hadn't started in a while, but in my mind I was ready to go.

It was a great feeling to be able to prepare all week for the game, and it was great to be in that position at that point in my career. I had all the confidence and I prepared myself. I worked extremely hard and got myself ready to go. I was excited about the opportunity and it was a great win. I felt good about my performance. I thought I was pretty efficient.

Coming out of the tunnel for the start of the game, you're excited and you're nervous. If you're not nervous, there's something wrong with you. But it was exciting. That first game is always exciting. You're starting out 0–0, and you want to get off to a good start. You want to get ahead of things from the get-go.

The team was ready, and we came out and played a very good game all the way around. To be a starting quarterback in that situation, that's why you play the game, to have that opportunity. I was thrilled, excited.

I remember our defense was amazing that day. It had (a franchise-record) 11 sacks. I remember it was just relentless against Bernie Kosar.

I had a touchdown pass and moved the team pretty well. I thought I played a solid game. It wasn't anything earth-shattering, but it was good enough. I got the game ball afterwards and all that. It was just a great day. I felt like I had proven myself. A lot of folks doubted I could go in there and win the game as the starter. There was just some uncertainty at the position at that point.

(The Colts led, 7–0, at the half and 7–3 in the third quarter, when Herrmann hit Reggie Langhorne with a 26-yard touchdown pass.)

I remember it was a corner route and it was 26 yards. Yeah, I remember it. We made the call, and the play opened up really well. The safety kind of

The Colts had lost eight consecutive season-opening games until quarterback Mark Herrmann led them to a 14–3 victory in the first game of 1992.

stayed in the middle of the field, and Reggie ran a nice route. I just put it on him. It was just a nice play.

In your mind, you feel like the game's going in your direction. You don't want to make a big mistake, throw a pick-6 or anything like that and let them back in it. We just kind of stayed steady and tried to move the chains and not take any big risks. That's number one in your mind, not making a big mistake that might turn the game around.

Like I said, it was a good day and I got a game ball after the game. Little did I know what was in store for me the next day. But that day was just awesome. I still have the football down in the basement somewhere. I've held onto a lot of that stuff.

The Aftermath

No one saw it coming. Not the season-opening win over the Browns, and certainly not the Colts releasing Herrmann the next day.

It remains one of the biggest public relations headaches in franchise history.

"We won the game, then the next day I'm gone. Let that swirl around in your head," Herrmann said. "Did I see it coming? Oh, gosh. Never. It totally blindsided me.

"You can only imagine. You start the opening game. You win the opening game for the first time since the move. You had a good game. You've got the game ball. What would make you think that would be coming?"

George was getting healthy. Trudeau's contract issues had been resolved. Herrmann no longer was needed.

Adios.

"Thinking back, it was not much fun," Herrmann said. "But looking back at it, you just have to laugh. That whole day was just such a shock.

"I believe (personnel director) Jack Bushofsky came for me. I was getting my lifting in before film and meetings. He said (general manager) Jimmy (Irsay) wanted to see me. The last thing I thought was I was going to get that pink slip."

He thought wrong.

"I felt good going into his office," Herrmann said. "Jimmy was sitting at his desk, and Ted Marchibroda was kind of standing back in a corner. I thought, 'Well, this is a little bit curious.'

"Jimmy said first off, 'Congratulations. You did a good job. You were a big part of that win.' Then he said, 'But we're going to let you go.'"

Herrmann gathered his belongings from his locker and drove home while battling anger and disbelief.

"I pulled in the driveway, and it was still the middle of the morning," he said. "I still couldn't believe what had just happened. My wife, Susie, said, 'What are you doing home?' I said, 'Well, you're not going to believe this, but they just released me.'

"Then we had a lot of questions. We're thinking, 'What are we going to do now?' I had a few teams call me, but I was just so devastated with how that thing ended."

Herrmann's initial reaction was to voice his displeasure with the decision and the organization that made it. Gradually, though, his stance softened. In fact, for a time he served as an analyst with the Colts' flagship radio station.

"In time I decided I was going to take the high road," Herrmann said. "I didn't really blast anybody. I decided to handle it professionally. I'm glad I did.

"It hurt me, no question. But as time goes by, you find a way to get past it. Jimmy has been nothing but great to me over the years. The whole organization has.

"Any bad feelings are long gone. You very rarely get to go out on your own terms. The way it ended for me was the cold part of this profession. I've always tried to look at the positives. If you have to end your career on a good note, that's one way to do it.

"Go out with a win that meant something."

CHAPTER 21

GARY BRACKETT

Linebacker 2003–2011
August 15, 2003, vs. Seattle Seahawks at RCA Dome
INDIANAPOLIS COLTS 21, SEATTLE SEAHAWKS 7

He was the guy nobody wanted all that badly. Not after being a two-time all-conference prep standout at Glassboro (New Jersey) High School. Not after walking on at Rutgers, earning a scholarship, and developing into a two-time MVP for the Scarlet Knights.

He was too short, too light, too this, too that.

The NFL, in general, and the Indianapolis Colts, in particular, weren't all that impressed with linebacker Gary Brackett, either. He wasn't among the 250-some draft-eligible players invited to the 2003 NFL Scouting Combine and wasn't among the 262 drafted.

The Colts signed him as an undrafted rookie on May 1, 2003. He was the longest of long shots as the team looked to fill in the bottom of its 53-player roster.

Brackett didn't flinch. Consider the mantra that's served him so well: It's not the size of the dog in the fight, but the size of the fight in the dog.

"Your whole life is people thinking that because you don't pass the 'look' test, you don't belong," said Brackett, generously listed at 5-11 and 235 pounds during his nine-year career with the Colts. "But when you turn on the film, they're like, 'Who is this guy making all those plays?' I've always been a smart football player. I always had a knack for the ball. For me, it was all about making plays.

"Turn on the film. The film does not lie. There are a lot of folks who look like Tarzan, play like Jane."

That tenacious attitude served him well when he reported to Anderson University for his rookie training camp.

"Coming in here as a free agent, they had the likes of Keyon White-side, Cato June, David Thornton was still around, Rob Morris was here . . . it was a tough time making the team, proving that I earned one of those fifty-three spots on the roster," he said. "I had a lot of stuff on my plate to deal with."

Attempting to earn a spot on an NFL roster was the least of Brackett's concerns. During a seventeen-month stretch that included his rookie season, he lost his father, Granville, to a heart attack, his mother, Sandra, to a stroke, and his older brother, Greg, to leukemia after donating bone marrow for a transplant.

"I faced so much adversity," Brackett said. "I just kept the faith. I knew how much my parents sacrificed, mortgaging the house twice to keep me in school and almost betting the farm on me. I was like, 'Man, I can't let them down. I didn't come this far to let adversity get in the way.'

"I played in their honor. Before games I would kiss my chest and point to the sky. I always told people (my parents and brother) had the best seats in the house. I always played like they were watching."

Act I was August 15, 2003.

Notes on Gary Brackett

Joined Colts: Undrafted free agent in 2003

Jersey: No. 58

Birthdate: May 23, 1980

Height: 5-11

Weight: 235

Games/starts with Colts: 116/86

Highlights: Perennial defensive captain. Appeared in 116 regular-season games, 86 as a starter. Started 11 of 15 postseason games, including Super Bowl XLI, when the Colts defeated the Chicago Bears, 29–17. Led the Colts with eight tackles in the world championship game. During nine-year career, produced 754 tackles and had at least 100 in five consecutive seasons (2005–09). Finished career with 12 interceptions and returned one for a touchdown. Also returned a fumble 69 yards for a touchdown against Houston in 2008 and recovered a fumble in the end zone for a touchdown at San Diego in '07. Forced a fumble at the goal line by Pittsburgh running back Jerome Bettis in a '05 AFC divisional-round playoff game. Appeared in 44 games at Rutgers and was team captain last two seasons.

The Game

By Gary Brackett

It was 2003, my first year there, man. Rob Morris was injured in the preseason in the Chicago Bears game. Jim Nelson breaks his hand. We had me and Keyon Whiteside left. They put me in as the replacement for Jim. That second game of the preseason, we played the Seattle Seahawks. I started the game, so I got to run out of the tunnel as the defense got announced. I started the game and we were off.

For me as a kid growing up, that's one of the things that always stood out in my mind to do one day. You know (PA announcer), "And at linebacker, Gary Brackett." For me, it was just outstanding to run out of that tunnel and hear your name over the PA. To actually be in that moment was something special. Just two weeks before that, I was fourth string, right? Now, I'm actually starting in front of all those fans.

It was one of those surreal moments. I always said if my career ended there, I at least would have lived out my childhood dream. That was it, man. I came out of the tunnel, heard my name announced on an NFL field.

During warm-ups, I was out there stretching on the field, and I looked up in the stands and I see a (jersey) number 58. I was like, "Man, that has to be for somebody years ago." He turned around and it had my name on the back. I'm sure there were only one or two in the stands for years. Nobody knew who I was from Adam.

The funny part was not only did the fans not know who I was because I'm a first-time starter in my rookie year, but half the team probably still doesn't know who I am. I'm running out of the tunnel and people are clapping, and they're probably like, "Who is this kid?" I can remember how nervous I was. I was like, "Please, don't trip and fall."

I remember I had a pretty good game. (Defensive coordinator) Ron Meeks was very complimentary after the game. I always had a knack for playing in third down and nickel packages. I guess I was an upgrade because I was faster in the open field in our cover-2 scheme.

I believe I had a sack or a quarterback hurry. I know I chased around (quarterback) Seneca Wallace a couple of times back there. I had a couple of tackles (four).

Linebacker Gary Brackett overcame being a walk-on at Rutgers and an undrafted free agent with the Colts before coming out of the tunnel and being announced as a starter.

I played the same system in college, so I felt very comfortable in the huddle. Rob was a great player, but I don't know how great of a huddle leader he was. For me, when I stepped into the huddle, there was no nonsense. I was like, "Hey, eyes on me. Eyes up. This is the call. Everyone get it? Understand?" I think everyone was yearning for that type of leadership. Guys kind of gravitated toward me.

Some people can play sideline-to-sideline, but it's about who can be a leader, who can play hurt, who can we depend on or who can be on board when we make an adjustment at halftime and be able to go out there and execute it. That's what makes good players great, or a guy who plays two years in the league play nine years. He was able to fight through some of those things.

For a lot of guys, it was just a preseason game. It meant so much more to me. It was about seizing the moment, seizing the opportunity. If I hadn't been prepared in 2003—during the offseason or during training camp—I'd have never made the roster. It was a pivotal moment and a pivotal game for me. First, I was a special teams player and I took pride in that. But in the NFL, it's fifty-three guys. You're an ankle sprain away from being a starter. I was given the opportunity and I proved I could do it. That really led the coaches to have a great belief in me that I could be a starter.

I walked on at Rutgers. I was undrafted and signed with the Colts. I take pride in how I got here, no question. People see you now and they're like, "You did what? You played in the NFL for nine years? Yeah, right. C'mon." Well, the checks have already been cashed. I don't have to prove anything anymore.

The Aftermath

The guy nobody wanted all that badly hung around and hung around and hung around.

Brackett's persistence led to a nine-year career in Indianapolis during which he appeared in 116 regular-season games, 86 as a starter. He also appeared in 15 playoff games, starting the final 11.

He was the perennial defensive captain, the mortar that held everything together.

Call Brackett an overachiever if you must, but he responded every time the Colts called on him. He knew only one way to approach the game: head-on.

"I lived in the moment when I played," Brackett said. "I appreciated every practice that led to the game that led to the winning streaks that led to the playoff wins that led to the Super Bowl. I really enjoyed the journey and what it took to stay on top and play at that high level.

"When I was doing it, I took my job and my career very seriously. It was a great nine years. I developed some really good friendships that will last a lifetime. Man, it was all about getting your opportunity and making the most of it.

"I did that."

Brackett always remembered how he got his break. An injury kept the players ahead of him on the depth chart out of the lineup. He stepped in.

And once entrenched as the starter, Brackett was loathe to relinquish his position. During one six-year stretch, he started at least 12 games each season.

"You know how the NFL works," he said. "All week in practice (prior to the Seattle game), I was running with the starters because Rob was hurt. I started the next three games, as well. Rob Morris came back two weeks early from his four-to-six-week injury, and he's the guy again. It was like Wally Pipp (replaced by New York Yankee legend Lou Gehrig). Don't drop your glove. Don't give up your spot.

"As a starter, you don't want anyone to see your backup guy play. Understand? You realize they're liable to take your job. You don't want to see that. I was like that when I was a starter. 'Nah, I'll play hurt. I don't want my backup out there.'"

CHAPTER 22

CATO JUNE

Linebacker 2003–2006
October 17, 2005, vs. St. Louis Rams at RCA Dome
INDIANAPOLIS COLTS 45, ST. LOUIS RAMS 28

The Indianapolis Colts, circa 2005, were in the midst of something special. So was Cato June, their third-year linebacker.

For just the fifth time in franchise history, the team opened a season with five consecutive victories. June was a defensive catalyst. During that rapid-fire start, he piled up 43 tackles. He intercepted three passes and returned two for touchdowns.

"It was a magical time for all of us," June said. "When you're talking about having success and with the consistency we had, you just don't see that a lot.

"Winning and having success became an expectation for us. That got to be our mentality. We expected to win, to be successful."

Few could relate to the level of success enjoyed by June. During his four-year career with the Colts, they posted a 50–14 regular-season record—12–4 three times, 14–2 in '05—and reached the playoffs each season. They advanced to the AFC Championship Game twice and captured the franchise's first world championship in over three decades with a victory over the Chicago Bears in Super Bowl XLI after the '06 season.

"It's crazy when you think about 12–4 being our worst record when I was there," June said. "It was a great thing to be part of.

Notes on Cato June

Joined Colts:	Sixth-round draft pick in 2003, 198th overall selection.
Jersey No.:	59
Birthdate:	November 18, 1979
Height:	6-0
Weight:	227
Games/starts with Colts:	56/45
Highlights:	Named Pro Bowl starter and was second-team All-Pro selection after 2005 season. Finished the season with 109 tackles and team-high five interceptions. Became the only linebacker in franchise history to return two interceptions for touchdowns in one season. Had 399 tackles during four-year career and posted at least 100 in each of last three seasons. Starter for Colts' 29–17 win over the Chicago Bears in Super Bowl XLI after the 2006 season. Signed with Tampa Bay as an unrestricted free agent after '06. Appeared in 89 games, 73 as a starter, during seven-year career that included stints with Colts, Buccaneers, and Bears.

"I couldn't imagine being part of a losing situation. I had never been part of that. Not in high school. Not at Michigan. Not in the NFL."

Yet that five-game winning streak to start '05 was in jeopardy when the St. Louis Rams visited in mid-October. The Rams brought a lackluster 2–3 record into the RCA Dome but bolted to a 17–0 first-quarter lead.

Then, the magic returned.

The Game
By Cato June

We played St. Louis on a Monday night, and there were just a lot of things that stood out to me. They jumped out on us pretty good. I got a couple of picks, a couple of big plays in that game, and I probably should have scored twice. I'm not saying we won because of me, but I definitely contributed at a great level. To me, that's memorable because I continued to play well.

My family was there. A couple of my buddies were there. I remember Chris Perry, who was playing for the Bengals at that time, happened to be at the game. I mean, everybody's watching.

When you go into a stadium and you've got tickets (for family and friends), we always used to check out where our guys were. You had to know where everybody was sitting. I wanted to know who to point to, so you had to know where they were. You had to know where your folks and friends were.

I just remember getting a pick and catching the eyes of my people. It was like, "Yeah, I'm feeling it right now." It's an awesome feeling. As a player, sometimes you get into a zone where you feel like the game has slowed down to you. You understand exactly what's going on. You know the plays that are there for you to make, and you're able to make those plays.

(The Rams led, 17-0, early in the second quarter, when June sparked the comeback with an interception of Marc Bulger.)

The first (interception) was a second-down play. (Torry) Holt ran a deep "dig" route off play-action. It happened just like we had practiced it. I was getting more depth in our "hook" drops because of the deeper routes they ran. When you get a great read, you feel like the quarterback is throwing you the ball.

I remember we had great film study that week. I had my keys down. I had it all figured out. It was like, "These are the plays that you can probably make." That week in practice, we knew St. Louis liked to run a couple of Viking routes, which had the inside guy clear. They ran their "digs" deeper than normal. Typically it's 12 yards, and they ran their "digs" and comebacks 14 yards, maybe 15. That was one of our keys. "Hey, we've got to get deeper in our drops because we knew they ran deeper 'dig' routes." We had help from our safeties.

With film study, you can really get on a roll. You can get on a good roll or a bad roll, and at that time I was on a really good roll. I was getting a bead on balls, picking off passes. I ended up getting two in that game, which is an awesome feeling, especially for a linebacker. I called myself a semi-linebacker. I was a DB at heart. I was a safety at Michigan.

After I got the pick, I had my little dance, and I'm going to celebrate a little bit and have some fun. It's amazing when you actually catch the eyes or connect with somebody in the stands. You're talking about 60,000 people at the RCA Dome, and you're able to connect with them. It's a great feeling. Amongst a crowd of roaring, crazy fans, you're able to connect individually with people who came to see you. I'm not talking about 59,990 people who are screaming for you. I'm talking about the 10 or so you've got there, the ones that were wearing my (No. 59) jersey.

It's just a different connection and an awesome feeling.

(The second interception came against backup quarterback Jamie Martin in the third quarter, with the Colts leading, 24–20.)

It just felt great to make some plays that really turned that game around. I had two picks in the previous game, as well, but you don't really go into a game thinking about that. I'm not going into a game thinking, "OK, I'm going to get two picks." I'm going into a game thinking I'm going to make plays. But I knew, "Hey, if they throw that check-down to Steven Jackson, I'm going to pick it." You watch your film and you get comfortable. That's what I always told the young guys: understand your opponent better than they understand you. If you understand what they're doing or what they're trying to do and how they're trying to attack you, you're ahead of the game. At the end of the day, it's about being in the right position and doing the job when you have the opportunities.

Anytime you're in that prime-time game and you make plays, ones that can be "forever plays," it's a great feeling.

I also remember that game because I had the privilege of playing against one of my idols. Being on the field with Marshall Faulk, man, it was amazing. You talk about Hall of Fame guys, that's Marshall Faulk. You take that for granted when every day you're out there with Peyton (Manning) and Marvin

Linebacker Cato June and the Colts' defense sparked a 45–28 win over the St. Louis Rams in 2005. June did his part with a team-high 11 tackles and two interceptions.

(Harrison) and Edgerrin (James) and Reggie (Wayne). That greatness becomes a part of who you are. In my opinion, Marshall was the best running back ever to play the game. He could do it all. You don't take that lightly.

So when you sit back and think about what might have been your best game ever, shoot, I had two picks against Marshall Faulk's team. At that time, (the Rams) were still on fire and still very high-powered. They came in and were beating our tail.

Then we turned it around.

The Aftermath

The come-from-behind victory over the Rams stretched the Colts' winning streak to six. It reached 9, 10, then a club-record 13 to open a season before perfection ended with a 26–17 loss to San Diego.

"That was our best team," June said. "That might have been one of the best Colts teams ever. We had an awesome team.

"People say, 'Well, you guys won the Super Bowl (in '06),' but I tell them our best team was the year before that. It wasn't even close. The best teams don't always win a championship."

The Colts, 14–2 and the AFC's No. 1 seed, lost their first playoff game at home against the Pittsburgh Steelers, 21–18. It was difficult to discuss at the time, but the franchise never fully recovered emotionally after coach Tony Dungy's son, James, passed away on December 22.

"The greatness in Tony Dungy was he was in a situation that's unthinkable," June said. "But he was able to press through it.

"I'll never forget that year. We were unstoppable. We weren't just beating people. We were dominating people like New England did when they went 16–0. We lost to the Steelers and we're there the next day for our exit physicals and cleaning out our lockers and everybody still was in shock.

"We couldn't believe it was over. But it was. Even though we didn't win it, it says a lot about the organization how we handled the situation with coach and how we came together. That team always will be remembered. The bonds you create when you face an adverse situation are just priceless."

CHAPTER 23

RAY BUCHANAN

Cornerback 1993–1996
November 6, 1994, vs. Miami Dolphins at Joe Robbie Stadium
MIAMI DOLPHINS 22, INDIANAPOLIS COLTS 21

When collegiate and NFL personnel experts looked at Ray Buchanan, they saw a rangy, ball-hawking safety.

The player in question dreamed of honing his skills at one of the more flamboyant positions.

At the University of Louisville, Buchanan "wanted to play corner. I wanted to play wide receiver."

Coach Howard Schnellenberger listened and even allowed the ultra-confident freshman to prove he deserved to play cornerback for the Cardinals.

"After seeing me get roasted outside a couple of times, it didn't look good," Buchanan said with a laugh. "I didn't have the footwork outside down yet.

"They put me at free safety and used my speed. That allowed me to roam free and use my instincts."

The Indianapolis Colts noticed Buchanan's impactful four-year résumé at Louisville—15 interceptions, 13 passes defended, six blocked kicks—and selected him in the third round of the 1993 draft.

They were convinced they had added someone who would emerge as a solid pro safety. He appeared in all 16 games as a rookie and started the final five at free safety. In his first NFL start, Buchanan intercepted

Notes on Ray Buchanan

Joined Colts: Third-round draft pick in 1993, 65th selection overall

Jersey No.: 34

Birthdate: September 29, 1971

Height: 5-9

Weight: 193

Games/starts with Colts: 61/50

Highlights: Set a Colts single-season record by returning three interceptions for touchdowns in 1994. Led the team with eight interceptions that season, which is tied for sixth-most in team history. Finished four-year Colts career with 16 interceptions. Signed with the Falcons as an unrestricted free agent after the 1996 season. Saw action in 184 games, 165 as a starter, during 12-year career. His 47 interceptions are tied for 47th-most in league history. Had at least one interception in each of his 12 seasons. Named to Pro Bowl in 1998 and started for Atlanta in Super Bowl XXXIII. Three-year starter at the University of Louisville.

a Scott Secules pass with less than two minutes remaining that sealed a 9–6 win over the New England Patriots. He would lead the team with four interceptions.

"My rookie year, I came in hungry. I wanted to start. I wanted to play," Buchanan said. "I was already mad I got drafted where I did. I dropped to the third round, and I felt like I had something to prove.

"I just played special teams and came in on nickel at safety or started a little at safety, not corner. Then they started to trust me more."

Buchanan yearned for more. He yearned to be an NFL corner.

"I wanted that so bad," he said. "I knew I could play the position. I was looking at Deion (Sanders) and how flamboyant Deion and some of the guys that came before me were.

"At that time, Deion was a hero of mine. I was like, 'OK, if I can't play offense, I might as well try to get the ball anyway I can.' I had that type of energy. I wanted to make a difference."

He wanted to be "Big Play" Ray Buchanan.

The transformation finally occurred in November of 1994, against Hall of Fame quarterback Dan Marino, no less.

The Game

By Ray Buchanan

During practice that week, I'm starting at safety. But I'd go out there and work on my footwork with the corners. (Veteran) Eugene Daniel started to pour positive energy into me. He used to say, "Man, your feet are so quick. You've got some real good feet." I took that to heart. He told me, "You've just got the instincts."

I started to believe Eugene. It was like, "All right!"

I finally got called on in the fourth quarter against the Dolphins and Dan Marino. They said, "Ray, you're gonna go play corner" because things weren't going well for us. Dan was lighting us up.

I remember getting this surge of energy. I was so excited. It could have been the other way around. Some guys might think, "Uh-oh, that's Dan Marino." Not me.

On that very first pass, I looked at Dan Marino and he looked at me. He noticed I wasn't in the middle of the field (at safety). He noticed I was at left corner. I knew the ball was coming. I just knew. He sort of had this big smile and kind of winked at me.

I know I didn't smile back at him. He smiled and I was like, "Oh, shoot. OK." Funny thing is, he noticed me right away. It was like, "If they're going to put you out there, I'm going to test you right away."

(Buchanan intercepted Marino's pass intended for Mark Ingram and returned it 28 yards for a touchdown that gave the Colts a 21–12 lead.)

It was a deep out and I sat on it. I had nice footwork, read it well, and broke fast. That was my first interception for a touchdown. I saw Ingram's hands dropping and saw the ball coming out of my peripheral vision. Dan was actually throwing the ball in my direction.

I moved back to safety after that because we had to go back to our nickel package. In our nickel, I couldn't play corner because I needed to be at the safety spot. On one play, Dan ended up splitting me and Jason Belser for a touchdown to O. J. McDuffie.

They came back and ran an out-and-up on me. They knew I was squatting on routes. They ran a double-move on me and beat me a couple of times. But, hey, that's Dan. He does that to you.

He became "Big Play" Ray Buchanan after the Colts moved him from safety to cornerback midway through the 1994 season.

(Miami rallied for a 22–21 win on Pete Stoyanovich's 34-yard field goal with four seconds remaining.)

We didn't finish that day, but that game right there is what really set it off for me when it came to encouraging me now to know I could play the position. The coaches were pretty enthused about that.

I proved I could play corner. I proved they could trust me. It took practice, then doing it in a game. Coaches want to be able to trust you, but you've got to be able to prove yourself. Some guys have that instinct and they just know. The Colts just allowed me to do it.

I was thankful for it because right after that, it was like interception after interception after interception. I got on a crazy roll. Eight picks (on the season), three for touchdowns, something like 28 pass breakups. It was crazy.

It's all about making the most of the opportunities you actually have. You don't have anything to lose. What's the worst that could have happened to me? They move me back to safety? I knew when I stepped out there at corner, I had to have faith in myself and believe I could go out there and do it.

At that position, you win some and you lose some. One thing you want to do is win your share of battles and let the coaches know they can trust you.

That's especially true when you're on the outside. I call it being on Gilligan. You're out there on an island like that. You're out there by yourself. Guys are counting on you. You've got to go out there and take care of your responsibilities. If you're man-to-man, you've gotta play tight coverage. If you're playing zone, you've gotta take care of your area. You do that, and guys start respecting you.

After the Miami game, I was a guy who always wanted to shake somebody else's hand. That was me. I always respected the older players. It was like, "Wow, that's Dan Marino. I've gotta go shake his hand." Or, "Wow, that's Jerry Rice. I've gotta go shake his hand."

After the game, I believe I did go look for Dan. I wanted to shake his hand. I wanted to shake a legend's hand.

The Aftermath

In retrospect, Buchanan appreciates the path that enabled him to build a 12-year NFL career that included stints with the Colts, Atlanta Falcons, and Oakland Raiders.

He appeared in 184 games, 165 as a starter, and his 47 career interceptions are tied for 47th-most in league history. Buchanan had at least one interception in each of his 12 seasons. The eight he notched in that transformational 1994 season are tied for the sixth-most in a season in Colts history, while the three he returned for touchdowns remain a single-season record.

Buchanan earned a Pro Bowl with the Falcons in 1998 and was instrumental in their reaching Super Bowl XXXIII, where they lost to the Denver Broncos.

"I'm very thankful for what the league provided to me and what it meant," he said. "You learn so much from the game.

"I look back at my life and just say, 'Wow.' I just think of all the different changes the coaches made to where I actually became the person I am, the player I was. Everything started to add up. When you're playing and coaches make a decision and put you in a different position, sometimes you don't recognize why. You don't really see it or appreciate it until you get done.

"It totally makes sense now."

CHAPTER 24

JIM SORGI

Quarterback 2004–2009

January 1, 2006, vs. Arizona Cardinals at RCA Dome

INDIANAPOLIS COLTS 17, ARIZONA CARDINALS 13

In stark contrast to the iron man at quarterback was the ever-changing nature of Peyton Manning's backup.

From Manning's rookie season in 1998 through '03, there was Kelly Holcomb and Steve Walsh and Mark Rypien and Brock Huard. The Colts even kicked the tires on Cory Sauter, Mike Quinn, Doug Nussmeier, Billy Joe Hobert, and Roderick Robinson by having them on the active roster at some point during that six-year window.

Stability arrived in 2004 in the person of Jim Sorgi, a sixth-round draft pick out of Wisconsin. He worked behind Manning for the next five-plus seasons, until an injury to his right shoulder in '09 essentially ended his career with the Colts.

Sorgi remains the answer to a trivia question: During Manning's 18-year career, who served as his backup the longest? Yep, it was Jim Sorgi.

"I'm happy about that," he said. "They chose to keep me around for six years. There were a lot of guys that backed up Peyton for his first six years. They kind of came and went.

"I'm proud of the fact he thought enough of me to want me around as his backup and the coaching staff and the organization thought I was doing a good enough job to keep me around."

Notes on Jim Sorgi

Joined Colts: Sixth-round draft pick in 2004, 193rd selection overall.

Jersey No.: 12

Birthdate: December 3, 1980

Height: 6-5

Weight: 196

Games/starts with Colts: 16/0

Highlights: Has the distinction of serving as Peyton Manning's backup—six seasons—longer than any other quarterback. Appeared in 16 games during six seasons and played extensively off the bench five times. Finished career with 89.9 passer rating by completing 99 of 156 passes for 929 yards with six touchdowns and one interception. Led Colts to two season-ending victories when Manning played sparingly—17–13 against Arizona in 2005 and 23–0 against Tennessee in 2008. In those two games combined, he completed 42 of 60 passes (70 percent) for 385 yards with two touchdowns and one interception. Started 17 of 32 career games at Wisconsin. Completed 288 of 519 passes for 4,498 yards and 33 touchdowns. Was Badgers' career leader in passing efficiency when he graduated. Started 12 games as a senior, passing for 2,251 yards and 17 TDs.

The job came with its perks, most notably working alongside one of the greatest quarterbacks in NFL history.

"It was the greatest job in the world because of what I learned from him," Sorgi said.

But there also was a downside. Manning notoriously took the vast majority of repetitions with the starting unit during practices. The backup—Sorgi—handled the scout team that prepared the starting defense for the upcoming opponent.

"Yeah, he took all the reps and I got all the scout team reps," Sorgi said. "He did share the 9-on-7 reps. There would be one day he would take them all, then the next day he would take half and I would take half."

Manning's approach would change, though, whenever it became apparent the backup likely would play in the upcoming game.

"If he knew I was going to play in the game or if there was a chance I would play in the game, I would take at least half if not most of the reps that week in practice," Sorgi said. "Peyton always felt like the guy that was going to play in the game needed to be prepared.

"I totally agreed with him."

The Colts opened the 2005 season with 13 consecutive wins before the San Diego Chargers ended their shot at perfection with a 26–17 decision in mid-December. That left closing games at Seattle and against Arizona in the RCA Dome, neither of which could impact the coming weeks. At 13–1, the Colts already had clinched the AFC South and the No. 1 seed in the playoffs.

However, the final two games of the regular season were anything but inconsequential. Two days before the Seahawks game, coach Tony Dungy's son, James, passed away in Tampa, Florida.

"It was decided since there was no more perfect season, let's rest our starters," Sorgi said. "We had everything locked up, so what's the point? I knew I was going to get a lot of playing time the last two weeks.

"Then, Coach Dungy's son, James, passed away. I remember getting the news, then flying down with the team to attend the funeral and him not being there when we played the Seahawks in Seattle on Christmas Eve.

"We came back home the following week and played Arizona to wrap up the season. We were surprised coach Dungy came back for that game."

It wasn't just another game.

The Game
By Jim Sorgi

I remember the Arizona game like it was yesterday because it was Coach Dungy's first game back. We played with a little extra want-to for him. Not that we wouldn't play with want-to anyway, but there was something extra that day. It just meant a little more.

Normally that type of atmosphere, with everything wrapped up and playing an opponent from the NFC that didn't have a winning record, you would have thought it would have been a very, very quiet, let's-just-enjoy-the-game crowd. But the return of Coach Dungy that week from what had just happened kind of amped it up a little bit. The crowd got into it.

I don't think the crowd really felt like we had much of a chance to win a ballgame if Peyton and the starters were not playing. So as that game went along, as we were getting momentum, we were moving the ball, we were scoring touchdowns, we had a lead . . . the crowd kept getting more and more into it. By the end of the game, when our defense made that stop and got that fumble recovery, it was pretty wild. The crowd was just going crazy.

After we won the game, I remember Mike Doss grabbing the game ball and taking it over to the sideline and giving it to Coach Dungy. It was a special, special game. It felt good to be part of a game that might not have had meaning in terms of wins and losses and who's going to be in the playoffs and seeding, but just in terms of winning a ballgame and getting us to a 14-win season.

Going into the game we knew we had a tough task. Arizona wasn't great that year (5–10 coming into the game). But they had a pretty good offense with (Larry) Fitzgerald and (Anquan) Boldin. Josh McCown was their quarterback and he was playing pretty good. They played a 3-4 defense and they did a lot of moving around and a lot of blitzing. They had Adrian Wilson at safety and he would come a lot on blitzes. There was a lot of checking and moving the protection to pick up a certain side of the defense where the blitz was coming from. I remember that week being pretty mentally stressful in terms of preparing for what we were going to see as an offense.

That's why it was important the backups got more reps that week in practice. We knew we were going to play the majority of the game

180

Backup quarterback Jim Sorgi led the Colts to a 17–13 win over the Arizona Cardinals in one of his rare extended appearances.

against Arizona. You actually knew what you were doing on the practice field was going to correlate to the field and you were going to be able to use it against an opponent. That was awesome.

(Manning made his 127th consecutive start before giving way to Sorgi after one series. Sorgi completed 20 of 30 passes for 207 yards and touchdown passes of 18 yards to Troy Walters and 14 yards to Ben Utecht.)

It was fun. We knew we weren't going to get a whole lot of playing time going into the season unless something happened to one of the starters, so getting that chance at the end of the season, we wanted to play well. We knew we were playing for our jobs. We knew we were playing for next season, to show everybody what we could do. If it wasn't with the Colts, it would be with another team. We wanted to put good film out there. We did that more often than not.

That game, I remember the Troy Walters touchdown. It was a double move of some sort. We were getting the blitz, we picked it up, they went "man" (coverage) and I think Troy ran a slant-and-go. I hit him in the corner of the end zone. Utecht caught a couple of passes. One of the balls should have been intercepted, but one he took and turned it up the sideline and took it in for a touchdown.

There was one play where Adrian Wilson came on a blitz and I kind of scrambled to my right. He grabbed me and just threw me down. I remember hopping up and saying, "You've got to hit me harder than that." I was just doing the normal trash talking on the field, but my hand was just throbbing. I got back to the huddle and I'm like, "Oh my God." As it turns out, I found out I had a little broken bone in my right thumb.

It was just one of those good battles. I actually had a guy on the other team, (nose tackle) Russ Kolodziej, that I played with at Wisconsin. It was fun.

We put up 17 points that day, but our defense played a great game, holding them to 13 points. Our defense did a great job of getting turnovers, making stops, especially against that offense that had some pretty highly-touted receivers. We probably wouldn't have won that game without our defense. Great, great job. We did what we had to do.

(Arizona trailed, 17–13, but took possession at its own 11-yard line with 7:28 remaining. The Cardinals' 17-play, 88-yard drive fell one yard shy when linebacker Rob Morris recovered a McCown fumble in the end zone with 13 seconds remaining.)

I'm standing on the sideline thinking, "Please just get that one stop." They show Peyton (in the '06 AFC Championship game) kind of sitting there (late in the fourth quarter) and kind of praying. Well, that was me against Arizona, a 5–10 team at the time, Week 17. That was my Super Bowl.

They had a 1st-and-goal at the 10, a 2nd-and-goal at the 2, then at the 1. To get that turnover was just incredible. And for Mike Doss to get the ball and hand it to coach Dungy was something special.

The Aftermath

As it turned out, the performance by the Sorgi-led backups against the Cardinals was the final highlight of '05. After enjoying a first-round bye, the Colts were stunned in the divisional round by the Pittsburgh Steelers, 21–18, at the RCA Dome.

"I was surprised with all the emotion we had that we didn't go on," Sorgi said. "We all know what happened in the Pittsburgh game.

"I felt that was a really good team we had that year."

Many believed the '05 Colts were better than the '06 squad that won Super Bowl XLI.

"We just had talent all over the place and things had kind of lined up for us," Sorgi said. "I guess it just wasn't meant to be. That was another of those opportunities lost during those years."

CHAPTER 25

BEN UTT

Guard 1982–1989

September 2, 1984, vs. New York Jets at Hoosier Dome

NEW YORK JETS 23, INDIANAPOLIS COLTS 14

The divorce was as public as it gets and still resonates intensely in Baltimore.

Dig through the archives from 1984 and cue up the video of those hours that spanned late March 28 and early March 29. It's hard to remain dispassionate at the sight of those Mayflower trucks, packed with every scrap of paraphernalia and the storied history of the Colts franchise, lumbering out of the team's Owings Mills (Maryland) headquarters and heading to Indianapolis.

The city of Baltimore was stunned by what it viewed as owner Robert Irsay's ruthless betrayal. When the shock subsided, rage set in. Tread lightly around those who have neither forgotten nor forgiven.

The city of Indianapolis celebrated as it joined the NFL fraternity. It had built a 60,000-seat Hoosier Dome at a cost of $77.5 million, but it needed an occupant.

"There was a hunt going on for the Colts franchise because (Irsay) wanted to move, so I said, 'Let's get into the hunt,'" former Indianapolis Mayor Bill Hudnut said. "There were two or three reasons Irsay had to leave. One, they hadn't renewed the lease. Two, attendance was down, way down. Three, Memorial Stadium. Bart Starr told me one time Memorial Stadium was known as the ash can of the NFL.

"Four, the media was not only hounding Irsay, but treating him rather badly. I always say Baltimore lost the Colts. We didn't steal them."

Jim Irsay, the owner's son and team's general manager, conjured up an interesting comparison when he considered the Colts' arrival in Indianapolis.

"I always kind of talk about the Beatles hitting America," he said. "It was this incredible time of going from a difficult situation to being so welcomed. It was a special time. When people really look at the facts, things really deteriorated. Both sides didn't handle it well. It got past the point of no return."

The Colts played their final game in Baltimore on December 18, 1983, a 20–10 victory over the Houston Oilers. A crowd of 20,418 was scattered around the 60,000-seat Memorial Stadium.

"The last couple of years in Baltimore, things were pretty dicey," said guard Ben Utt, whose Colts career spanned two cities. "The fans in Baltimore were glorious fans, but there was a little bit of a love-hate relationship with the team."

The Colts stumbled while taking their first step in Indianapolis, dropping a 23–14 decision to the New York Jets on September 2, 1984. The sellout crowd of 60,398 rocked the Hoosier Dome.

"It was really amazing," Utt said.

Notes on Ben Utt

Joined Colts:	Signed as a free agent January 18, 1982
Jersey No.:	64
Birthdate:	June 13, 1959
Height:	6-5
Weight:	286
Games/starts with Colts:	110/95
Highlights:	Started at least 12 games in five of last six seasons with team, including all 16 in 1988 and '89. Starting left guard in 1985, when the Colts led the AFC in rushing (152.4 yards per game), and appeared in 16 games, eight as a starter, in '83, when team rushed for a conference-best 168.4 yards per game. Latter figure is third-highest average in team history. Four-year letterman at Georgia Tech. Offensive captain as a senior. Played in the 1980 Blue-Gray Game and Senior Bowl.

The Game
By Ben Utt

I remember we won our first game in the Hoosier Dome. We beat the Giants in the preseason. But the first regular-season game was against the Jets, and we weren't able to get that one.

As an offensive player, you knew they had Mark Gastineau and they've got Marty Lyons. They were still the New York Sack Exchange. Those guys were pretty good. Whenever you played the Jets, you never had to go looking for them. They were right there in your face. It always was a street fight.

We knew the Jets were a team that really got after you. They had something like three or four sacks. Those guys were some really, really great competitors.

From that standpoint, it was a hard-fought game. It's just that offensively and defensively, we weren't that good. We had some very good players. We had Curtis Dickey, Chris Hinton, Ray Donaldson, Randy McMillan. It was Ron Solt's rookie year. We had Kevin Call, Ray Butler, Barry Krauss, Donnell Thompson. It also was Eugene Daniel's rookie year, and he ended up being a great player.

Like I said, we had a lot of talent, but things just didn't come together the way we had hoped.

(Linebacker) Cliff Odom and I were the captains for that game. The atmosphere was incredible. I remember people saying Indianapolis was a basketball town, but I thought it had a good football background. Notre Dame was just up the road. When the PA announcer came on during games, we couldn't hear on offense because the crowd kept doing the wave when we had the ball. They had to learn when to do it and when not to do it. You know, do the wave when we're on defense. There was an education process, and there might have been some hints along the way.

It was a great community. They just loved having the team there. They were so supportive for a pretty average-to-poor football team, especially from a wins standpoint.

The game was a struggle, back and forth. And what I remember is that place was just packed. It was packed for every game. We just didn't get it done. Shoot, that whole '84 season wasn't a good season. Not a lot of wins.

Guard Ben Utt helped the Colts transition from Baltimore to Indianapolis in 1984.

The Aftermath

The Colts' first steps in Indianapolis were shaky, so there was nowhere to go but up.

The early growing pains—a 12–36 record in the first three seasons, three playoff appearances in the first 15 seasons—finally gave way to prolonged success highlighted by a trip to Super Bowl XLI after the '06 season that produced the franchise's first world championship since 1970.

While it's difficult—and undoubtedly painful—to believe, the Colts actually have spent more time in their new home than their old haunts. The 2016 season marks their 33rd in Indianapolis, where they've played 541 games overall, including 30 in 17 playoff appearances. The Colts' history in Baltimore: 31 seasons, 438 games, and 15 playoff games in 10 appearances.

"When you think about it from today's perspective, boy, what a great move if you're the Irsays. A great move," Utt said. "At the time, Memorial Stadium was a great place to play because of all the great ghosts who played there – Johnny Unitas, John Mackey, Raymond Berry, and all those guys. But it was a very run-down place. The locker rooms were terrible for visitors and the home team.

"What's kind of great is Indianapolis now has established itself with Peyton's legacy and the players they've had. Great guys like Jeff Saturday and Andrew Luck. Knowing Jimmy Irsay the way I do, it's great to see how things have gone. We share the same birthday—June 13, 1959—so we're birthday buddies. What a great success story with where things are now."

Utt experienced the end of one city's claim to the Colts and the beginning of another's. His loyalty is divided geographically, but not at its core.

"I'm a Colt," he said. "As a player, you want to play, right? You strap it on and play whether it's in Baltimore or in Indianapolis. Teams have moved in the history of sport.

"When I mention to young players now that I played two years in Baltimore, they're like, 'So, you played with the Ravens?' I tell them, 'No, there was a team in Baltimore before them.'"

EPILOGUE

The circle of Peyton Manning's NFL life, one that included a notable four-year arc in Denver, closed on March 18, 2016, at the Indianapolis Colts' complex.

How appropriate.

That's where it began 18 years earlier, when Jim Irsay introduced his fan base to its newest hope for excellence. The Colts invested the first over-all pick in the 1998 draft on an All-American quarterback out of Tennessee and then followed his footprints for the next 14 years to historic success.

March 18, 2016, was about reflection, and recognition.

Irsay admitted it was strange watching Manning lead the Denver Broncos to a pair of Super Bowl appearances and one world championship "without the horseshoe on his helmet."

"Not easy," he said. "We kind of feel like he's ours.

"I can't say enough for what he has meant to this franchise, to this city and state. You just simply run out of words thinking about how much No. 18 means to us.

"Actions are the most powerful things in life, more powerful than words."

The subsequent actions carried long-term ramifications.

No other Colt ever will wear Manning's No. 18 jersey. It marks the eighth retired number in franchise history.

Manning's recognizable 18, Irsay stressed, forever will be "proudly sitting next to No. 19 (John Unitas), who I know you have so much affection for."

Also, the team will erect a statue of Manning outside Lucas Oil Stadium, the state-of-the-art facility whose construction could be traced to his presence.

"It's not too often you build statues of people, particularly in their lifetime," Irsay said. "So much deserving."

Manning was moved, appreciative.

Indianapolis Colts owner Jim Irsay and Peyton Manning shared a historic moment as the team retired Manning's No. 18 jersey.

More than that, he was home.

"This is the team that I wanted to play for," he said. "I was glad that y'all drafted me."

"I'll always be a Colt. This is where I played 14 of my 18 years, and I had a chance to play with some great teammates. I'm extremely honored to be a part of those teams and to play with so many great players and coaches."

Then, Manning took everyone on a sentimental journey.

From Peyton Manning's press conference on March 18, 2016:

I can remember when I signed with the Colts, I missed three days of training camp. I did not want to miss any of camp but kind of learned the business side of things. May have missed some more time if Kelly Holcomb didn't run into Marshall Faulk on a handoff in training camp. Marshall Faulk turned to somebody and said, "Get that rookie quarterback in here." And I was on a commercial flight into Indianapolis that night and met Tom Condon that night at St. Elmo's. It was his third trip to St. Elmo's that night, which has got to be a record. And then came over here the next morning, signed my contract, and drove up to Anderson with Bill Polian and was at practice that afternoon.

The very first preseason game, my very first pass I throw a 5-yard (pass) and Marvin Harrison ran 48 yards for a touchdown. I was thinking, "This NFL is easy. You just throw a short pass to Marvin Harrison and he runs for touchdowns." Which is pretty much what he did the entire time he and I played.

I can remember a preseason game, going down to Mexico City against the Pittsburgh Steelers and my center, Jeff Saturday, catching a little "Montezuma's revenge" and me asking (offensive line coach) Howard Mudd if we can be in the shotgun a little more that evening.

I remember Reggie Wayne's first touchdown against Houston on a tipped ball. Kind of an uneventful game, but I remember it.

I can remember Colts fans, just the amount of jerseys they wore in the stadium, in the old RCA Dome, more than in any other stadium in the league, in my opinion.

I remember Tony Dungy's press conference and meeting with him and learning some of his phrases and expressions. "No excuses, no explanations" and keeping those with me throughout my entire career.

I can remember the calmness of Coach Dungy in the AFC Championship, down, 21–6, and (him) saying, "We're fine. We are fine."

Also remember him saying all week that we were not going to kick the ball to Devin Hester. Then some players saying, "No, we can get him. We can get him. Let's do it. Let's do it." And the one time Coach Dungy actually changed his mind, well, that didn't work out so well on the kickoff, but we sure did win the game and that sure was a special night.

I can remember the fans' celebration here in Indianapolis after we beat the Patriots in the championship game. There was nothing quite like it in downtown Indy.

I remember that miracle night in Tampa. And I remember getting texts and emails saying, "Hey, sorry about the loss. Keep your head up. Better luck next week."

I can remember the painful losses against the Steelers and the Saints.

I can remember walking off the field with Reggie Wayne, who was from New Orleans. Two guys that just got beat by their favorite team growing up. But I was glad to be there with Reggie, and I was glad we bounced back after the Steelers and won a Super Bowl the next year.

I remember the old AFC East, right? The original AFC East. Head coaches that year were Jim Mora, Jimmy Johnson, Bill Parcells, Wade Phillips, and Pete Carroll.

I remember the RCA Dome and how loud it used to be and watching (Robert) Mathis and (Dwight) Freeney speed up the field and Bob Sanders torpedo some guy right in the back.

I remember some deep communication philosophy talks with Howard Mudd on protection.

I remember coming over here on Tuesdays as a rookie and throwing out routes to Mike Mays out here because I couldn't complete this out route to the left.

I remember arguing with Jeff and Tarik (Glenn) over whether we should be running the ball more. Healthy conversations on the sideline. Kind of always felt outmanned by that.

I can remember Jim Mora's "Playoffs?" press conference. I'm sure people enjoy it, (but) not exactly a fond memory for me. The reason he said that is because I threw four interceptions in that game against the 49ers, so I don't enjoy seeing that quite as much.

I remember many a quarterback meeting with Kelly Holcomb and Brock Huard and Jim Sorgi, Curtis Painter. Those guys helped me so much.

I remember (Ken) Dilger and (Marcus) Pollard, just always enjoying breaking the huddle having Dilger and Pollard at each of my tight end spots.

I remember Mike Vanderjagt kicking two 50-yard-plus field goals in the snow in Denver, and our flight back got canceled. We stayed up all night at some crappy hotel in Denver, and we all enjoyed it.

This is a football town, and as good a football town as any. These fans love their team and they're talking about football in February, March, April. It's year-round now. It was fun to be a part of that kind of transformation.

There were so many people that were part of that, Jim and Bill and Edgerrin, Marvin, this long list. It was fun to kind of witness that first-hand. It's something I'll always cherish being a part of.

I did not get shorted at all in anything football-wise in really my 25 years if you go to high school and college. I got my football fill as a player . . . I have no regrets because I've worked so hard and prepared as hard as I could to get ready to play and so you cannot say that I was shorted.

I think I'll be OK.